HOW TO MARKET, ADVERTISE AND PROMOTE YOUR BUSINESS OR SERVICE IN A SMALL TOWN

By Tom Egelhoff © 1998 Eagle Marketing

Published By Eagle Marketing
P.O. Box 271 Bozeman, Montana 59771-0271
406-585-0219
Toll Free 1-888-550-6100
Bozeman, Montana City Business License # 45916

email: tommail@smalltownmarketing.com
website: http://www.smalltownmarketing.com

Printed In Bozeman, MT USA
By Speedy Print

HOW TO MARKET, ADVERTISE AND PROMOTE YOUR BUSINESS OR SERVICE IN A SMALL TOWN

By Tom Egelhoff

He who finds a wife finds what is good and receives favor from the Lord."

- Proverbs 18:22 NIV

To my best friend in the world, my wife Janet. For standing by me all these years and always having absolute faith in me when, at times, no one else did.

Special thanks to Professor Mike Reilly, Marketing Department of Montana State University for writing a wonderful preface and for encouraging me to jump into the deep end of the pool and write this book.

Mike and I met while presenting a marketing seminar in Bozeman, to a convention of Montana Educators in 1993. I had just moved to Bozeman. At lunch I mentioned that I had been toying with the idea of writing a small business marketing newsletter.

Mike, in a special style he has, pointed out that a newsletter was a lot of work, "Why don't you just write a specialized book on marketing?" he said. Sure, just write a book. About what? Marketing has been done to death.

The Small Town 101 chapter of the book details how I was inspired to write about small town marketing. I hope you enjoy it.

Table Of Contents

INTRODUCTION

By Mike Reilly
Professor of Marketing - Montana State
University

When Tom Egelhoff asked me to write the preface to his new book on Small Town Marketing, I had no idea he was actually going to blame me for the whole project. However, while reading the introduction I discovered that he attributed the notion to write a small town marketing book to a conversation we had several years ago. While I don't remember having that conversation, and therefore can plausibly deny all responsibility for the end product, I was interested in reading the manuscript.

I can bluntly say, as a marketing professor for over 20 years, that this is the most practical and usable help for people to market small businesses in small towns that I've ever seen. By using lots of examples and talking in non-technical language, Tom has made the secrets of marketing a business in a small town intellectually available to a wide audience. There are lots of good ideas here, even for folks with lots of experience.

As you read through the book, I would encourage you to apply the concepts to your business.

While you'll find some outstanding ideas that you can apply immediately, the real benefit of the book will come from better understanding the perspective that is needed to successfully operate any business in the challenging environment of small towns. As Tom clearly points out, small towns typically don't provide a continual flow of new customers. Tactics that will work successfully in larger cities often fail miserably. Market research data, information on the audience of media, demographic information, economic data, and a variety of other resources that can help guide decisions in more populated areas are typically sketchy or absent in smaller towns.

Despite this, small business owners make marketing decisions daily that can have substantial positive or negative impact. Prior to this book, there has been little in the way of guidance. I am very familiar with most of the academic and popular literature on marketing, and find little of it to be of much use for most of my small business consulting clients, because it is broad, general and frequently describes tactics that may be appropriate for a large manufacturer, but difficult to translate to a small business scale.

Tom's book does an excellent job of adapting traditional marketing thought and technology to the unique problems of small towns. If you're marketing a small business in a small town, there is no better source of information available.

I intend to distribute this manuscript to small town clients for whom I provide marketing consulting service. I think you'll find it to be helpful and informative.

Mike Reilly
Professor of Marketing
Montana State University
Bozeman, Montana

Small Town 101

The Miracle Mile

This book was conceived, in part, because of a Powerball Lottery winner and a Rand-McNally Road Atlas. You may remember the name Leslie Robins, the teacher, who won the $110 million Power Ball Lottery. It seems that Robins lives within walking distance of a lottery winners "Miracle Mile" in Fond du Lac, Wisconsin. This "Miracle Mile" has produced more than $150 million dollars in winners.

Upon reading this rather interesting article, I pulled out the Rand-McNally to see exactly where this town is located. I was amazed, when I reached Wisconsin, to discover that there are so many small towns on the map that they barely fit within the borders of the state.

After finding the miracle mile, I quickly decided not to jinx those already living there by packing up the wife and moving to Fond du Lac. Instead, I continued to look through the Rand-McNally to see if other states had similar numbers of small towns. To my surprise—many did not. California, for example, is the most populated state in the country, but they have a much lower ratio of small towns to large ones than say Illinois or Missouri. Eastern Kansas has many towns; western Kansas relatively few. My home state of Montana has the highest concentration of towns in the Western portion of the state.

OK, so what? Every state has a higher number of small towns than large towns, and what difference does it make where they're located? Well, the size of the town, and how it is located in relation to larger cities, can have a great influence on your business success or failure.

How Small Towns Work

Let me use my own hometown of Bozeman, Montana as an example. In larger cities, throughout the nation, goods and services are available in large numbers. If you want carpet for your home, just open the Yellow Pages and there are many to choose from. In a small town the choices are more limited. If there is a large city nearby, I need to make a decision. Is it worth it to me to travel to the big city to make my purchase? If it is, what about service? Will the company come out to my little town if I have a problem? How much service will I need and is it worth it? Are the savings, if any, worth the drive?

Drive a lot, Save a little?

Bozeman is a town in southwestern Montana with a population of 32,600; During the summer the town shrinks to 22,000 when Montana State University is not in session. The nearest large city to the West is Butte, 82 miles away, population 37,000. To the East is the city of Billings, 142 miles away, population 88,000, the largest city in Montana. Do people make the long drives from Bozeman to shop in these cities? Yes...They Often Do!

Before you question the sanity of Montanans, keep in mind that distances in Montana are perceived differently than other areas of the country. With 147,000 square miles and a population of only 800,000 people, the freeways are virtually empty by most big city standards. That's 5.4 people per square mile. This makes the drive a family outing and the scenery on both drives is, to say the least, spectacular. Many business people must travel to these towns to meet with manufacturers and suppliers. It's the only way they can do certain types of business.

The point I want to make is this. In a small town there is a certain amount of isolation and that can be very good for business. If you have the goods and services customers want and they feel they can do business with you, they will not make that drive, regardless of how beautiful it is. Best of all, the amount of competition is reduced. On the other hand, if you don't manage your business effectively they may well drive down the road to the bigger city.

The Social Graces

Another important point to keep in mind, small towns are more "socially oriented" than large cities. You not only know your next door neighbor, but probably everyone on your block including all the kids.

There are positive's and negative's to this. The positive is that many neighborhoods treat new arrivals as a great excuse to have a party. Cakes and cookies are baked, cookouts organized and a block party breaks out. These are the people that will help you ease into your new business environment. They will be happy to take you to their service clubs, introduce you at church functions and help you "fit in".

The negative is that some areas of the country see newcomers as more crime, more traffic, higher housing prices, more government and the deterioration of their once peaceful village. Forgetting, all the while, that at one time they may have been new in town themselves. Some of these people will have to be "won over." Here are some suggestions:

1.) Find the friendliest person in town and build on him or her.

2.) Don't say anything negative about your town or the neighborhood. Be positive about your new home.

3.) Don't tell people how good everything was in your last hometown. You may be invited to go back.

4.) Learn as much about the town as possible, before you move, so you can take part in conversations. Subscribing to the local paper is a good source of information. Don't quote the newspaper. Although nearly everyone reads the paper, few will admit the paper fairly represents their side of any issue.

5.) Avoid talking about politics and/or religion until you know your listeners quite well. Find ways to get involved in the community as soon as possible. Join clubs such as the Rotary, Kiwanis, Lions, Elks, etc. Attend the church of your choice regularly. It's not the purpose of this book to espouse any religious ideology, but in my opinion, this is the most non-threatening place in any town to make friends. The whole purpose of church is to welcome you to the fold and help you.

If you have special skills, make sure the local Chamber of Commerce knows about you. Every day people contact the Chamber for recommendations of goods and services.

Can you teach your skill? Contact the nearest Adult Education organization. They are always on the lookout for qualified business experts. I teach classes in sales, computer layout, marketing and advertising, business cards and brochure design. Each of these classes has led to business contacts and jobs. I also make valuable business contacts with class members, whose expertise and contacts in their specific areas can be valuable to me in the future.

Expertise...Have you got it?

If you've owned or managed a business in a large city, the chances are you will have a higher level of expertise in your field than most of your local peers who have not operated a business in a large city. Before those of you who own a business in a small town throw this book across the room, let me explain that last statement in more detail.

I don't mean to imply that just because you have a business in a small town you don't know what you're doing. There are plenty of very successful business owners in small towns. It's just that there are certain advantages in larger cities that just aren't available in smaller towns.

Let me use a sports analogy here. The tougher the competition, the better a team becomes over the long haul. The very fact that tough competition exists forces a business owner to get tough and lean, or cease to exist. The level of competition is almost always higher in larger cities. There are more stores providing the same goods and services at lower prices. The employee pool is larger and more experienced. The advertising options are more extensive. The promotional opportunities are better. And, the successful business owner can quickly learn marketing secrets from some very talented people who don't make a lot of mistakes.

Does this mean if someone from a city opens a business you should close yours? Of course not. An established business will always have some advantage over a new one unless the newcommer is a national chain or well known name that can generate a quick customer base.

Learn the ways of a tiger.

So, how should I compete against all this expertise? Well, I could move your business to a major city for a couple of years and then move it back. A better idea might be one a college professor of mine taught and it's very simple. "To catch a tiger, learn the ways of a tiger."

In other words, learn as much as you can about your business, your competitors and your customers. One of the best places I know of is trade magazines. Whenever I would read about a marketing consultant in a business magazine, I would call the person and talk as long as he or she would stay on the phone. I remember talking to a business consultant in Hawaii for over two hours. The expense of the phone call was a small price to pay for the knowledge I received.

Another great way is talking to any sales people who call on you. Remember, they also sell to your competitor and may let valuable information slip during casual conversation. Business today calls for more and more expertise. One thing is certain, small town or large, knowledge is power.

KNOWLEDGE IS POWER

Read as much as possible about your business or profession. Will Rogers once said, "All l know, I read in the newspaper". And he made a living telling it to audiences around the world.

Subscribe to as many trade magazines as you possibly can and take the time to read them. A great many are free to qualified companies. "I don't have the time to do all the things I need to do now, let alone read magazines". Well, that's OK. When your business fails you'll have plenty of time to read. Find the time. If you spend just 20 minutes a day reading something about your industry, in one year you will know more than 75% of the people in that industry.

Talk to a knowledgeable expert in your industry at least once a month. Learn the ways of a tiger.

Now lets get started on your marketing plans.

Section One: Chapter One
The Small Town Marketing Plan

Getting Started

Now that we've established a small town perspective, from the Small Town 101 section, let's create some marketing strategies for your business.

What is a marketing plan anyway? "I thought I just needed a business plan." A marketing plan is a part of your overall business plan. I usually recommend that 30% of your business plan should be devoted to how you are going to market your business. Your marketing plan is one major area that investment bankers take a real close look at before lending you any money. They are very curious how you will attract customers, make sales, make a profit and pay them back on their investment in your business.

You will use some of the information from the business plan in your marketing plan, but the marketing plan is usually its own entity within the business plan.

If you don't have a business plan started yet, do that first. S.C.O.R.E. (Service Core of Retired Executives) can offer free help to get you started. Find them at the Chamber of Commerce. Also, check out your local Small Business Development Center. If you are in a smaller town that lacks these advisory groups, create your own set of coaches by taking retired business leaders out for coffee and pick their brains in a methodical manner.

Once you have your financial statements and projections together you can move on to the marketing plan.

Where do we start? We start with you. You need to sit down and really look at yourself and your business as you never have before. This is the most difficult part of the marketing plan. We never let anyone really see the "real us". You must be completely honest with yourself about who you are and where you're going.

A little information is a dangerous thing.

Before customers enter into a relationship with a business, they quite naturally, want to know something about that business. That's where a marketing plan starts.

Who Are You? Why would I want to do business with you? In addition, you need to know every aspect of your business before you can prepare your advertising and target your customers. Here's how to start.

If you were looking for a job and saw an ad in the classifieds, what questions would you ask yourself? The first question would probably be— "Am I qualified to do this job based on the job description." If the answer is yes— you put together a resume and request an interview to present your qualifications to your prospective employer.

Business is no different. You need a resume (or complete description) of your business that can be presented to qualified customers (your target market) in the form of an advertising message. This "resume" is sometimes referred to as a business review or background review.

In the next chapter, I'll give you suggestions for a few things that should be included in your business resume.

Chapter Two:
Step 1: Business Resume:
Who Are You?

Ask yourself the following questions as though you were a customer of your business.

1.) How long have you been in business? If yours is a new business, what experience do you have in this field? As a customer, would I feel comfortable that you can do the job, or provide the level of service I am accustomed to? Are special machines needed in the production of your product? Could importing materials put the company in jeopardy if they weren't available? Will training be required of employees to produce the products? What are the company's - long and short- term goals? Are there existing sales goals? What is your mission statement or company philosophy?

2.) Who are the principals in the business? What qualifies them to start or operate this business? What special skills do they have? What is their education or training in this industry? Are they members of any associations in this industry? Is city or state licensing required for this business, and if so, have they complied with all local regulations?

3.) What purchase rates or buying habits are related to your product or service? Would I buy it once a week, a month, a year? What is the demand for your product or service? Is it seasonal? Is it hard to use? Are there multiple users? Are there going to be heavy users of your product? What percentage of your total sales will they be? Is your basic industry growing or shrinking? Is the customers base in your city or county growing or shrinking? Is your product a luxury or a necessity?

4.) What about awareness and attitude about your product or service? Does your product harm the environment in some way? Is it fun or useful? Is your product well known or will the public need to be educated about how to use it? Are you the next Hula Hoop or Pet Rock?

5.) Most businesses have some form of competition...how about yours? Who is your principle competition? (Ask all the questions in #2 above about the competition.) How big are they? What can you do that they can't do? Can you specialize in areas they can't? If you are competing against a large public company (i.e. Wal-Mart, Costco, etc.) buy some of their stock. You'll receive their annual report, and as a stockholder, a lot of information will be available to you. Warning: Do not skimp or gloss over this business resume section. It will be very valuable later on when we deal with positioning your business.

6.) How's your pricing compared to the competition? Can you be competitive or are you going to have to ask a higher price? Is the lowest price always the best? Of course not. Customers place a value on products based on their perceptions of that product. They base those perceptions on the information they get from you and other sources and comparisons. If I said, CD player, a dollar figure jumps into your head based on advertising you've seen or input from friends or any of 100 different sources.

7.) You can't have a business without customers. You must identify your target market. Who are the people most likely to use your business? Their age? Sex? (Most books refer to this as gender... Gender is language, not people...sex is people...look it up). Occupation? Martial Status? Home Ownership? TV shows they watch? Newspapers and magazines they read? Average household income? Education? Lifestyle? Number of children? All the stuff you find on a warranty card when you buy a vacuum cleaner or a blender. In addition, do some secondary research. For example, if you are lucky enough to be in a town large enough to have a library, it should have census information for your state and county. This will give you a profile of the average person living in your county.

The Chamber of Commerce may have the demographics of your city. Start with these and be prepared to adjust your business as needed. A good library will have a copy of the Rand-McNally Commercial Atlas and Marketing Guide. You'll find retail sales data for your state and county. What did people spend on food? Housing costs? Clothing? Automobiles? It's a great thumbnail source of information about people in your state or county. I'll cover how to reach these folks in the advertising section coming up later in the plan.

Who are the "end users" of your product? For example, I ask my wife to pick up some beer when she goes to the store. She makes the purchase, but she is not the end user of the product, I am. If I recommend a brand name I influence the purchase, if not, she will probably get something "light" or on sale.

8.) How much business is really out there? In a small town this becomes very important. I grew up in a small farm town in Illinois. The population was 5,200 people. Yet, in a three block area, there were 6 gas stations. These stations all stayed in business during my grade school to high school years. That's twelve years in business. When we create a business plan we must know if there are enough paying customers to support our business. Forget the competition (not entirely) for the moment. Each one of those gas stations shared a customer base of at least 5,200 total customers to survive. Some customers only went to one station for all 12 years, some went to all stations for 12 years, and the rest a combination of the two. The point is; each station needed X number of customers per day, week, month, year, to survive in this market.

Could a seventh station go in this market and survive? The answer is yes. Would it be easy, the answer is no. If you were going to open a new gas station in this market you would need to know the answer to three questions:

One: Can you develop new customers who do not go to any of the other stations? (New people moving to town, people just turning 16 and getting a drivers license.)

Two: Can you take customers away from your competitors? (People unhappy with the service, unhappy with the quality of the product, unhappy with price.)

Three: Can you develop enough of both to make a living?

If the answer to all three questions is yes, I would advise you to continue constructing the marketing plan. Please keep in mind we are only in Part One of a 10 Part Plan. This example with the gas station is greatly simplified for demonstration purposes. There are a lot more things that have to happen for that seventh gas station to survive than just those three questions . If the answer is no, then I would advise you to stop and regroup.

This process is commonly called a Sales and Market Share Analysis. How many sales; and how many people for the business to survive? I will tackle this in more detail as I go through the rest of the marketing plan.

9.) Next, let's talk about distribution of your product or service. What is your service area? The whole town? The whole county? The state? Is it delivered? Do customers pick it up? Can or does it need to be shipped? Will you need delivery vehicles? A shipping budget? FedEx account? UPS? Is it an intangible item: Life Insurance? Office cleaning? Groomed dogs? Do customers come to your place of business or do you go to their home or business? In small towns you may be required to travel to rural or farm areas for business. How much of this will be necessary and what is the cost of that travel?

10.) How is the product or service going to be sold? Where do customers of your product shop now? Will this change in the future? Will you need to hire salespeople? Will it be sold off the shelf in stores? Mail-order? Internet? 800 number? Do you know what the cost of sales of the product or service will be? If you have to pay a commission to a sales person, that will certainly take part of your profit.

11.) If you are in a common industry like shoe stores, or construction companies, CPA's, real estate, etc. start studying how these companies are advertising in your area. Are they on radio? TV? Newspapers (what section what days?) In San Diego (not a small town, I know), construction and remodeling companies comprised almost all the ads in the weekly newspaper TV listings. Why? Because it hung around the house all week.

Now that we have the answers to these questions, it's time to move on to Chapter Three and find out what we do with this information and how to begin to construct our marketing plan.

Chapter Three:
Step 2: S.W.O.T.?

Congratulations, you've finished your business resume and its time to see what we've got to work with. As you analyze your resume you should notice that you have Strengths, Weaknesses, Opportunities, and Threats. (S.W.O.T.)

Let's look at each part independently. Take one piece of paper for each of the items you listed in your business resume. Principals of the company, product awareness, competition, etc. Draw a line down the center of the page and list strengths and weaknesses on one side and opportunities and threats on the other. You need to go into great detail here. You must objectively look at every possible aspect of your business.

This will help you organize each component of your business and let you capitalize on each strength/opportunity and deal with each weakness/threat. The first part of our resume asked you to look at the people involved with the company. Are there problems? Lack of expertise? Experience? If there are problems how can you solve them or are they something you must live with. Can you deal with the problem immediately or are you going to have to wait for a solution?

Example: under product distribution, your product may be expensive to ship. This may cause a reduction in your profit. Is it a weakness? Arranging a contract with a local shipping company may be a way to make this area a strength. Or perhaps you will have to limit the expense by shipping only once a week while growing your business.

What challenges are short range, long range? Maybe you're working out of your basement and space is already a problem. How long will it be before you can afford commercial space? Can you trade services for commercial space? A cleaning company may clean the building in return for a space in the building.

These first two sections are by far the most important of the entire marketing plan. In the coming months, you will refer to these sections over and over again, as your market changes. Keep these work sheets in a handy place. Add and delete strengths and challenges as your business changes.

Chapter Four:
Step 3: Sales Forecasting

First Things First -
(How does the selling process really work?)

Before we move into setting sales objectives, I want to spend a moment showing you how the sales process actually works. Do you realize, in the academic world, there is no fully accredited textbook on selling that fully defines both the knowledge and skills needed to sell a product or service? There are no actual degrees in selling, nor are there measures of competence based on skills for the licensing of a person in the selling profession.

The life insurance industry has long had a reputation for having the best sales training of any industry. Life insurance companies are supposed to have the best-trained sales people. In 1965, over 80% of all life insurance was sold by fewer than 20% of the sales people. In 1990, 80% of all insurance was being sold by fewer than 15% of the sales force. Sales competence is actually decreasing rather than increasing.

Sales Competence

Every sales program has the same goal - to improve the competence of salespeople. Yet, to date, no books, training programs, or any other efforts have shown any overall measured improvements of salespeople's competence.

This should be the time you point out to me that you don't have a "sales force" so all this isn't really applicable to you. Wrong! If you deliver a product or service to anybody, you sell! And if you plan to be successful against your competition you better learn how the process works, and how to make it work for you.

So, why are most salespeople worse instead of better. One possible answer is two sales myths that I would like to debunk right now.

Myth Number One: If you want to make more sales, make more calls. Hustle is the name of the game.

Nothing could be further from the truth. I will agree that if you make 5 calls per day, day in and day out, to the right target market, something is going to happen and you will sell something. Let me show you a better way.

How to measure sales

Several years ago I worked for Victor Business Machines. At the time they were the number one manufacturer of adding machines and calculators in the country. They had a very simple sales philosophy. Every Monday, make 75 cold calls to businesses, door to door. That's a great way to start your week, huh? My objective of the 75 cold calls was to find 20 businesses that would allow me to place a machine in their business to try for a couple of days. Of the 20 machines placed, the national sales average, at that time, was 5 sales. seventy-five cold calls nets 20 placements equals 5 sales.

If I'm working this system, what are my objectives? Do I want to make 75 cold calls or do I want to make 20 placements? Right, I want the 20 placements. My goal is to make the 20 placements with as few cold calls as possible. That's where the real secret of selling comes in - Measurement.

Each Monday I would measure how many cold calls it took to make the 20 placements. If I got a "no", before I made the next call, I would review in my mind what happened with that call. What could I have done differently? How could I have overcome that objection? I had to constantly improve my initial presentation. Over time, I found I was only going to hear about a half dozen real objections. As I learned to overcome those my placement rate improved and I had to make fewer cold calls.

Next, I was expected to make 5 sales out of the 20 placements. At first, I was inexperienced, and I wasn't doing that. Once again, I had to measure what was going on with each demonstration and close. As my presentation, overcoming objections and demonstrating value improved, my closing ratio improved. So, what was my objective here? To make 5 sales or more than 5 sales? Very good, more than five sales is what I want to do.

So am I making more calls or am I working smarter? Go to the head of the class - Yes, working smarter. Only two things will improve selling competence: Increased specialized knowledge and information (product knowledge) and more productive selling skills (measuring what is going on with each sale).

Myth Number Two: Sales people work for you and company goals and monetary incentives will improve performance. Wrong! There isn't a sales person alive who works primarily to achieve the sales quotas of any company.

Salespeople work toward their personal individual monetary goals for themselves and their families: Sending kids to college, paying the mortgage etc. If the benefits to the company conflict with the benefits of the employee, which do you think will be most important to the employee? The company or their family?

Find the real motivation

If you want to motivate a salesperson positively, find out what they are interested in. What is their one overpowering burning desire? It may not be money. Some people just want to be appreciated for their efforts. What about the hourly clerk in the retail store? More money per hour to go to a job where your efforts are ignored by the boss? What's that worth? Most people, if given the choice, will give up cash for appreciation of their efforts. Hundreds of studies support this position. Read Tom Peters book, "In Search of Excellence".

Get Personal

Get to know your employees on a personal level. Support them and help them achieve their goals and they will move mountains. Encourage them to measure their efforts and teach them how to improve performance as a way of obtaining their personal goals. You'll keep good employees and develop a sales force to be reckoned with. Even if your sales force is only you.

1 Inch Drill Bit??

Why would I ever buy a 1 inch drill bit? So I can display it over the fireplace for all my guests to see? No, I buy a 1 inch drill bit because I want a 1 inch hole. I don't want the drill bit I want the hole! I want the benefit of the product. I don't buy a copier, I buy 1,000,000 copies over a seven year period. This is how you need to see your product or service before you present it to your customers.

Lets look at the Seven Selling Steps and how they work:

Step One: Greeting and Acknowledging the Customer

Your customer can purchase from you or your competitor and how you interact with them can have a strong impact on their decision. If you took a survey comparing the friendliness of people in small towns versus big cities, small towns would probably win hands down. It's a national perception that people in small towns are generally more friendly and go out of their way for folks. People in New York City, by contrast are perceived as rude, and for some reason seem to be proud of it. Courtesy is a skill you can perfect into a productive habit. Courteous persons have practiced being courteous and perfected that skill into a productive habit and are not even aware they are being courteous.

In contrast, aggressive and pushy people have formed those habits and are not aware they are aggressive and pushy. It is physically and emotionally impossible to be polite and courteous and aggressive and pushy at the same time. You can't be polite and courteous at work and not at home. It is either a habit you have perfected or it isn't. Start being as polite and courteous as you can all day every day for the next 21 days. Research says if you do something at the same time in the same way for 21 consecutive days, it becomes a habit.

How's Your Climate?

How is the climate in your town. No, not the weather climate. The friendly climate. What is the "standard average" level of people where you live? Polite and courteous or aggressive and pushy? For example, here in Bozeman, on a scale of 1 to 10 with 10 being so friendly strangers would loan you their cars, Bozeman is probably a 6. The population here turns over about every 7 - 10 years (mostly due to the weather). Every 6 or 7 years some -30 degree weather convinces some folks Arizona might be better. We get a lot of folks here escaping the big city for the "friendlier" small town. They sometimes bring the aggressive pushy attitude they learned in their former home to their new home.

Businesses here want to maintain a standard friendliness of 7 or above. If they can do that they know the majority of customers will take notice and hopefully remember how well they were treated compared to other businesses. In a large city, because of the large customer base, a company can lose a few customers and still do well. In a small town, with everybody knowing everybody else, it's much more important to make and keep customers. If you are an employee of a company and are reading this book, show the next few sentences to your owner, boss or supervisor.

Be a good listener

Listen up business owners: Customer service starts at the top. It doesn't start at the counter or the sales floor. It starts with you. How do you treat your employees? I promise you this - your employees will treat customers in the exact ratio as they are treated by you. If you constantly find fault with them, that attitude will be passed on to the customer. If they are proud of their position and performance and are appreciated and encouraged by management, that is also passed on to the customer. The better they feel about themselves the better they will treat your customers.

Have you ever eaten in a McDonald's Restaurant? Let's suppose you're on vacation. Someplace you've never been before and you spot a McDonalds®. How confident are you that if you go in its going to be pretty much the same as your hometown McDonald's®? Why, because all McDonald's® operate from the same manual of how they should look, sound, and cook. We expect a certain level of service from some businesses. We always expect our bankers to be in white shirts and ties. We don't expect the same from our mechanics. What should your customers expect from your business?

Question: How would you treat your very best friend if they walked in the front door of your business? Treat everyone that way because I'll bet your competition doesn't.

Last, but certainly not least, get the person's name if you don't know it and use it frequently during the initial interview. Most people aren't extended the courtesy of hearing their name at a business. Make yours the exception. As Dale Carnegie said, "A persons name, is to that person, the sweetest and most important sound in any language." If you don't believe that, try calling someone Bob who's name is actually Steve, and see how quickly they correct you.

Step Two: Discovering Customer Needs

How much can I stress the importance of this portion of the selling process. If you don't have what the customer needs you are wasting your time and theirs to continue with the process. If you don't discover customer needs immediately, it is costing you money in the selling process. Here's how:

I sold furniture for eight years. Early in my sales career I was taught many valuable lessons about the sales process. For example, when a customer asked to see a dinette set, 9 out of 10 salespeople took them to the area of the store where all the dinette sets were and start showing them to the customer. The correct way to make this sale was to first discover the customer needs by asking questions.

The type of questions you want to ask are called -open ended- questions. Open ended questions can't be answered by a simple yes or no. They require the customer to provide information.

 What kind of dinette set do you have now? What do you like about it? What don't you like about it? What about size? Shape? Color? Natural Wood Grain? Formica top? Vinyl seats? Fabric? Price range? As we collect the information we are adding and deleting merchandise in our minds that will fit the description of what the customer is telling us. Once we have that information we can say to the customer, "Based on what you've told me, I have three dinette sets that will meet your needs." "If you'll come this way we'll take a look at them."

What have you told this customer using this method? I'm not here as a store tour guide. I'm interested in you and I'm taking my time to find the right set for you. I don't want to waste your time showing you things that don't fit your needs.

Step Three: Selling Merchandise Benefits

Remember our drill bit. I don't want the product, I want the *benefit* of the product. Before we looked at any products I asked several questions and decided on a choice for them. They hopefully are thinking, "At last, maybe this salesperson has what we want and we can stop shopping."

Now, as I demonstrate the product, I will point out how the product fills each need, within the price range they said they wanted to spend. If I go to a product that is higher in price than they wanted to spend, then I need to justify the extra expense with some form of benefit that is of value to them.

Step Four: Addressing Concerns (More commonly know as, Overcoming Objections)

Let's go back to measuring for a moment. Remember, I mentioned to measure what happens each time you make or lose a sale? If you are getting a lot of objections you are not doing a good job in Step Two: Discovering Customer Needs.

There are two kinds of objections: Valid and Invalid.

No salesperson should make an effort to overcome a valid objection. A valid objection means the person does not have any need of the benefits of what is being sold or that the cost cannot be made to fit within his or her budget. This person is not a prospective customer.

An Invalid Objection on the other hand is almost always a request for more information. "Well, it looks good but I need to think about it before I spend that much." Translation: "You haven't shown me enough benefits to justify the price."

Objections should be welcomed. They are buying signals. "Help me buy your product." is what the customer is really saying. You haven't shown me the value yet. Don't ever show or talk about a feature unless you have a real benefit for the customer. There's an old adage among attorneys - Never ask a witness a question you don't know the answer to. It's the same with customers. If you don't know something, admit it, and get the answer for them as soon as possible.

Step Five: Suggesting Additional Merchandise

Most people at this point would probably go straight for the close. But this is an ideal time to suggest additional things that will enhance the sale for the customer. You can also use additional merchandise as a closing question. I'll tie the two together in Step Six: Closing The Sale.

What types of merchandise can you sell your customer? One of the most common in appliance sales is the dreaded "service agreement". That extra coverage to make sure the product performs as it's supposed to after the product guarantee expires. When I worked at Circuit City®, the national appliance retail giant, a percentage of our total sales had to consist of service contracts. The interesting thing about service contracts is, some people always buy them, some people never buy them, and everyone else falls somewhere in between.

To sell a service contract, we didn't start at the end of the sale as an add-on to the sale. We planted seeds during the sales presentation about service and how great the service is and it almost became an assumption that the customer would want the service contract.

In the car business, it was undercoating. In women's clothing it's the matching handbag, belt, shoes, etc. Add-on selling is certainly nothing new and can be almost automatic if done correctly. It is also commonly referred to as "suggestive" selling. Keep in mind that in suggestive selling, just as the other steps above, there must be a value or benefit to the customer to any add-on. Also keep in mind we don't want to cheat, manipulate, mislead or pressure the customer to ever purchase anything they don't want. If the value and the need is there, why would the customer not purchase?

Step Six: Closing The Sale (Asking For The Order)

Now is the time to close the sale. This is the most difficult function of the selling process for the inexperienced salesperson and probably the easiest for the professional. The overwhelming reason most people give for not buying a product - No one asked me to. No one asked me to buy the product. I almost fell over the first time I read that. Shouldn't that be a no-brainer? Shouldn't we be asking customers to buy our stuff?

Fear of rejection is pretty powerful. We will risk losing the sale before we'll face the disgrace of rejection. The reason for this is most salespeople wait for the customer to buy and if that doesn't happen they blame the loss of the sale on price, delivery options, any excuse they can think of except the real one: They did not ask for the order.

Let's explore how to ask for the order. The first step in the closing process is to make yourself familiar with what is called the "trial close". These are non-threatening questions you can ask the prospect that indicate where you are in the sale process.

An example of a trial close questions might be: "Would this color work in the room?" "Are you thinking of trading in your present car?" "How soon will you need this installed?" If this color won't work then asking for the order is useless. You need to return to Step Two: Discovering Customer Needs and get better color information and re-evaluate your product choices for this customer.

However, the customer exclaims with great enthusiasm, "This color would be perfect!", that's a pretty strong buying signal. You may want to go straight to the close here, or if you still think there are questions, ask another trial close question. If you get yet another positive response then the customer may just be waiting for you to take control of the sale.

My wife will tell you I hate to spend money on stuff we really need even if I know we need it. I will buy her clothes all day long and never think a thing about it. But buying a shirt or tie for myself, that's another story. I always justify that I can get by a little longer with what I've got.

My point is, I'm the type of person who wants to buy but if you don't ask me, you'll lose the sale. What can you do that will move me off the fence and get me to say Yes. Yes. Yes!

The most popular types of closes are:

1. The Assumed Close: Or Order Blank Close.

In this close you simply assume that you have a sale and begin to fill out the sales order. "What is the delivery address?" If the customer gives you the address, without objection, they have bought the merchandise.

2. The Major/Minor Close:

In this close, the customer makes a major purchase by answering a minor question. "Would you prefer delivery on Tuesday or Thursday?" "Thursday would be better for us." You just made the sale.

3. "Answer the objection" Close:

In this close you answer the customers objection and go to close one or close two above.

4. "Third person" Close:

This is a very strong close if the customer was referred to your business by a satisfied customer. You can relate how happy the friend is with the product, the service, the delivery and its a natural progression that they want the same level of satisfaction.

5. The "Ben Franklin" Close:

In this close the sales person takes a sheet of paper and draws a large "T" on it. On the left are the negatives of the product and on the right are the positives of the product and the reasons the customer should buy. Take notes during the questioning phase of Step Two: Discovering Customers Needs and put the very items the customer asked for on the right. The customer can quickly see that the advantages of having the product far outweigh the disadvantages of not buying.

6. "Yes Momentum" Close

Picture a huge boulder rolling down a hillside. At first it starts rolling slowly and gradually begins to pick up speed until it's rolling at breakneck speed. The increased speed is momentum. With our customer we don't want to increase the speed of our speech, but we do want to create a momentum of the customer saying yes, yes, yes, to a series of questions. We are looking for agreement from the customer that the benefits of the product will fill the needs and the momentum confirms that.

7. "What does it cost?" Close?:

In the case of an automobile, a refrigerator, or a fax machine, there are costs that are required to keep the product in operation. An automobile customer may be looking for the best gas mileage. What is the monthly cost of electricity to operate a refrigerator? Can your model cut costs? A fax machine will need toner cartridges and the cost per fax may be cheaper for the customer with your model. We all want to save money as long as we don't have to sacrifice the benefits of the product. So show value and you will have a sale.

8. "Bonus" Close:

Some customers just like to get a little something extra. Some type of bonus, such as free delivery, extra service, or some other incentive may make the difference for these customers.

9. "What will it take to get your business close?":

"Mr. Customer, I know this product will do the job for you." "I know you'll like it." "What do we have to do to get your business?" Shut up and listen. In many cases it might be some minor concern that you can easily take care of.

The other advantage: it lets the customer have some limited control of the sale. It also shows that you are willing to work with the customer and gives you added credibility in their eyes.

10. "Reduction to Ridiculous" Close:

If the customer is anything like me, you need to show me that my objections are just a smoke screen. I want the product but I just don't want to say yes. Don't insult your customer by saying their objections are ridiculous. You can show that in an implied manner by detailing each objection and overcoming it. Hopefully, they will see how silly they are being and make the purchase.

In the long run, what you're always trying to do with customers: Show them the disadvantages of not buying.

Step Seven: Assuring Satisfaction

Ever have buyers remorse? That sickening feeling in the pit of your stomach that you might have made a mistake in your purchase? You paid too much? Should have gotten the other one you looked at? Sometimes buyers need you to reinforce to them that they made the correct decision.

Operating a business in a small town demands that every customer must be a satisfied customer. There is a two-edged sword called "word of mouth" that can make or break a small town business. Positive word of mouth can be the best possible advertising you can get. If you react too slowly negative word of mouth can put you out of business quickly *and* permanently.

Follow-up on every sale is crucial. Make sure the customer is absolutely satisfied in every way with your business. Make it easy for your customers to complain about anything they're unhappy with. Most of us want to avoid complaints and confrontation with angry customers and we take the "They aren't going to get the best of me" attitude.

There always seems to be the fear that the unhappy customer will demand free product or service from you for life.

You must face these folks and resolve their problems and show them you are a fair and honest business they can have confidence in. These problems must be addressed as quickly as possible. If you ignore them they will fester and escalate into negative publicity or possible lawsuits.

However, customers rarely want to rip anyone off. If they feel they have been wronged, all they usually want is to be heard. They seldom have unreasonable demands.

Ask them to explain exactly what the problem is, then shut up and listen. Don't interrupt to make your points until they are finished. Restate their complaint back to them so they are sure you understand and have heard what they are saying. Then simply ask, "What would you like us to do to resolve your problem?" If you listen and refuse to argue you will find in many cases they will apologize to you for flying off the handle and thank you for resolving the problem... and you have retained a customer.

Nothing is more valuable than a satisfied customer, and they will help your business like nothing else can, by asking them for referrals to other customers. Can you use them in your ads or commercials? Testimonials in small towns are very powerful. The more respected the person the more powerful the testimonial.

Now that we know the basics of selling let's get back to sales forecasting.

Sales Forecasting

What are sales objectives? In a nutshell, they are what must be done to keep the doors of your business open. If you don't do enough sales you are out of business (unless you're the government). According to your business resume, that you did at the start of this plan, you say you can do certain things and have certain abilities. The next step is to translate these things and abilities into sales.

Determining Sales Objectives

How do we determine our sales objectives? I like to start at the end and work backwards. Remember the Victor Business Machines story told earlier? Seventy-five cold calls for 20 placements equals 5 sales. Our sales objectives must be based on the end result of what we expect our business to accomplish monetarily.

Our objectives must be challenging, yet attainable. The market must be of sufficient size to support the business (remember the 6 gas stations). All marketing programs are based in real time. We must set time specific goals for our sales objectives to be completed. We need both short (1 year) and long term (3-5 years) objectives. We must also consider projected profits. We must make sufficient plans to realize enough to pay the bills and hopefully pay ourselves.

Now, if you've been in business for a number of years you can use past performance as an indication of how your business is growing or not growing, as the case may be. Speaking of growing, I can't tell you how many business owners I've talked to who have told me, "I really don't want to get any bigger." I'll let you in on a little secret. You don't have a choice. I know you think you do, but believe me you don't. Your business will eventually take on a life of its own and it will do the dictating to you as to what you will or won't do. You *will* do it or you will be out of business.

Make some projections.

If you haven't been in business before, you are going to have to make some educated guesses and get some outside help. One place to start is the public library. You can start with the Encyclopedia of Periodicals. I don't care what kind of business you're in, there is a trade magazine or newsletter that covers it. These folks survey their subscribers about a host of topics. How do you advertise? What's your advertising budget? How do you promote your business? What are your business projections for the next five years?

Subscribe to as many trade magazines as possible. Some of them can be expensive. Write each one and tell them you are in the business and ask them for the qualifications of a free subscription. I have free subscriptions to Target Marketing, Direct Marketing News, Business Marketing, NetWeek, and Publish, just to name a few. It's in their best interest to provide free subscriptions to serious people in the business because those are the exact people the advertisers are trying to reach.

If you are new in business, another good resource is the Small Business Source Book. Your library should have a copy. If not they can surely borrow it from another branch. This book has helpful information about a large variety of businesses with ratios, budgets and other helpful information.

Next, the library also has a list of Associations. Again, almost any industry you can name has some kind of association. And what's the purpose of any association? To work for the success of the members of the association, of course. These people are also at your disposal to assist you with market research regarding your industry. You can also meet successful people in your industry who are more than willing to help you (unless they are a direct competitor of yours). Look for another city similar to your home town (preferably in another state). The next town is probably your competitor.

For Bozeman, Montana I use Boulder, Colorado for business information. It's approximately the same size as Bozeman, a college town, similar distances to other cities, similar housing costs and taxes, and forms of government.

If you were going to open a bakery for example, you would get on the phone and call some bakeries in Boulder and see if they would share with you what they feel the next 1 to 3 years are going to be like. Some will talk with you and some won't. Talk to the ones that will. Save their time, and yours, by making a list of the topics you want to talk to them about and go down the list. The conversation will go faster and the person called will appreciate your consideration of their time.

Business Costs

Next you are going to have monthly fixed and variable costs of operation. Fixed costs remain the same whether a single sale is made or not. Variable costs increase or decrease based on the number of sales made.

Fixed costs are things like the rent or equipment leases. Variable costs might be monthly shipping charges, cost of supplies, sales commissions; any expense that changes from month to month. If you aren't sure which they are, consider them fixed. Remember other things like insurance, maintenance, payroll, utilities, auto, and advertising costs to name just a few.

Break Even

When you have your costs under control you need to consider a break even analysis for each product or service you provide. The break even analysis assumes that average variable costs are going to remain constant for each product or service. This analysis is strictly internal. It doesn't consider things like competition or market demand.

What's the formula?

Are you sure you're ready for this? OK, stay with me here. Total profit equals the number of units sold multiplied by the selling price less the number of units sold multiplied by the total variable cost minus the total fixed cost. Pretty simple, huh? If P is profit, p is price, U is units sold, V is variable costs and F is fixed costs the equation would look like this:

$P=U(p-V)-F$

So, assume our bakery produces cakes and wants to sell them for $10.00 and we want to sell 1,000 of them. For this example our total fixed costs are going to be $7,700 and our total variable costs are $4.50/unit. (These numbers may not be accurate for the bakery industry) Our formula would look like this:

P=1,000($10.00-$4.50)-$7,700=$5,500-$7,700= -$2,200

What happened?

Instead of making money we have just lost $2,200. At break even the $2,200 number should be $0. We can't make money at 1000 units so how many cakes must we really sell to break even?

We know our fixed costs (F) are $7700, and the price (p) is still $10.00 and our variable costs (V) are $4.50/unit we do this:

(p) price minus (V) variable costs divided into (F) fixed costs or
$10.00 - $4.50 = $5.50 divided into $7700 = 1400 cakes.

If we maintain our price and expenses we need to sell 1400 cakes to break even. If we raise our price or reduce expenses we can sell less.

Some points to remember. The break even analysis does not show profitability. It will show some levels of profit at various levels of sales but sometimes profits must be thrown at company problems. Even though a product breaks even (or makes a profit) if all other goods and services don't, you could be in trouble. This is a guide to get you started. Good accountants are worth their weight in gold. Take this basic information to them and have them tailor it to your business.

Once you have the information as to how much it will cost to keep the doors open and the business viable we can move on to the next part of the marketing plan

Chapter Five:
Step 4: Who And Where Are Your Customers?

Finding the target

In this part of the plan you must identify the target market. Who are the people most likely to use our product or service. The smaller the town the easier it is. If you live in a town of 1,000 people or less the demographics of your city may have similar percentages of age, education, home ownership as large cities but the numbers are in double digits not per 100,000 population. If you live in a town of 1,000 or less and 750 are over the age of 70, on fixed incomes, and you're selling life insurance, you may be in trouble. They may want to buy but can they afford it? Can you sell enough to the other 250 to make a living?

Demographics of a region are very important to your business health. There must be enough potential customers in your city or county of the right age, income level, education, etc. to support your business. I worked with a company in San Diego to erect a sports complex where Major League Baseball players could conduct clinics for kids during the winter. The San Diego Union newspaper had a demographic study of the entire county. We were able to pinpoint the zip codes that had the largest populations of kids 8 to 13 years of age. Advertising targeted to those zip codes and those parents produced more customers than we could imagine. Several clinics had to be added.

Can you sell to the world? We have many businesses in Bozeman that don't make a dime selling to anyone in town or even in Montana. The majority of their business is done out of state. They just enjoy living here. If you live or have visited San Diego, California you may have gone to see a ball game at Qualcomm Stadium. Qualcomm has an office in Bozeman. Ross Perot's old company EDS has an office here. Gibson makes some of the finest guitars in the world here. If you play your local or state lotto, chances are the machine that prints the ticket and records your numbers was made here by Powerhouse Technologies.

As you can see, it doesn't really matter where your target market is as long as you know *who* they are. That's what it's really all about. Who are these people? Very simply they are a group of people with common characteristics.

The first step in target marketing: Determine if the primary target group will include purchasers, users, or both. Which uses the product the most? Who actually buys the product?

Step Two: Does your target group's demographics coincide with your present customers? Do adjustments need to be made?

Step Three: Is 67% of your business done by 33% of your total customers? If so, then the 67% users become your primary target market. The 33% your secondary market. For example: 67% of the beer drinkers are men but only 33% actually go to the store and buy it. Their wives do the shopping and purchasing. The men would appear to be the secondary market from a purchasing standpoint but they are actually the primary market. Confusing? That's what makes target marketing so much fun.

Have you bought an Arch Deluxe lately? What's an Arch Deluxe you ask? How quickly we forget. It's the McDonald's® flagship adult sandwich that once again proves there's no one in the cockpit flying this plane. McDonald's® spent billions becoming *the* family restaurant. How much are the playgrounds in the front of these places? When I see the playground out front, do I think I'm going into an adult restaurant? The Arch Deluxe, the McLean burger and other adult fare are dying a slow horrible death. You would think they would have learned from their "light and healthy" salad menu a few years ago, which also died a slow horrible death. People who eat healthy wouldn't be caught dead (excuse the pun) in McDonald's®. They're going after a target market, that past experience says, is the wrong market. What's next, the diabetic menu? It doesn't matter if you're big or small, the wrong market is the wrong market and in a small town the wrong market will end your business.

Let me show you the right way to do this.

1. Look at your total market:

Continually identify all types and categories of people, industries and others that might use your product or service.

2. Break It Down:

Break down your list of potential markets into groups that have common characteristics. For example, list people by professions or industries.

3. Analyze your markets:

Discover as much as possible about the groups you have segmented. What do they like? Not like? What do they want? What do they fear? Who do they buy from now? Why do they buy from them? How much potential does this target group have? How can you sell them?

4. Study the competition:

How do your competitors do it? What are they doing that is working in your market? Can you do something similar? Can you acquire some of their market share?

5. Prioritize:

Rank market segments by priority. Primary market should be the easiest to reach with the lowest investment and greatest expectation of return.

6. Do an in-depth market analysis of your top markets:

Uncover as much information as you can about your most likely customers, including what they read, what trends they are concerned about, and how they think. Who do they consider best in your field and why?

7. What forms of marketing are most successful?:

Studies show if people hear about your business or service four or more times they perceive you as credible. The fewer resources a company wastes (marketing to people who will never be prospects) the more it can invest reaching and selling to its genuine prospects. "How did you hear about us?" can help zero-in on ways to reach new customers. Flash-in-the-pan advertising is usually a waste of money.

8. Test Your Markets:

King Schools, in San Diego, California, is a company which sells video tapes that assist pilots in passing their pilots license exams. They sold the course for around $250.00 because that price beat out $199.00 and $159.00 in a test of three different markets. Customers who received information on the $159.00 and $199.00 course thought it was too good to be true, at that low price and didn't buy. You may find, what you thought was your best market, may be your second best market.

9. What do you have to do?:

How many customers must walk through your door or how many sales calls must be made before a sale takes place?

10. Choose your markets carefully:

Keep in mind that it's not how many target markets you can identify and open - its how many you can profitably penetrate, market to, and serve. Treat your target market as an open ended question, always changing and providing new information.

Finding your target market is a top priority. If you aren't selling to the right people you won't have a business long. The smaller the town the smaller the total customer base the quicker the death.

Chapter Six:
Step 5: How To Create A Plan
& Work It

Now that you know your target market the next step is to develop the marketing objectives and marketing strategies to reach them. Let's start by defining the two terms.

1. Marketing Objectives:

A marketing objective is what needs to be accomplished. It must be specific. It focuses on one singular goal. It must be measurable. There must be a specific time period: 30 days? 6 months? 2 years? Whatever the time, it must be specific. Objectives can also relate to specific parts of the marketing plan.

2. Marketing Strategy:

A marketing strategy details how an individual marketing objective will be achieved. It describes the method of accomplishment. Strategies are descriptive and tell how the objectives will be met.

Another example might be a football game. The objective is to win the game. The strategies are the plays we use to accomplish this. The objective has a specific time: the length of the game. It focuses on one specific goal, win the game. The strategies on the other hand change as the game goes on due to injuries, weather, score of the game, field position, the play clock and other variables.

Suppose you have a baby products store and your sales objective is to increase dollar sales 10% over the previous year. We have a specific and measurable goal, 10% - one year.

Some of the strategies we might use to accomplish our goal:

Your primary target market might be pregnant women and new mothers with infants up to three years of age. One possible secondary target market might be new grandparents. So you'll want to focus your advertising efforts on reaching these two groups. You need to know from your target market research what newspapers they read, TV shows they watch, magazines etc. Also keep in mind that you can't ignore your existing customers, you must keep their loyalty.

Put your marketing department, which may consist of only you, to work on a marketing plan to reach the target markets. Perhaps a mailing to all new mothers in the area. How do you find them? Birth records at the county court house. Plan a big sale for the month most babies are born in? If you didn't know, its September. My personal theory is that September is nine months after Christmas and New Years Eve, when we all seem to love each other the most.

You could package a ready-made baby shower plan with everything needed to put on a successful baby shower. More people might give showers if there was some indication they would be successful.

Next, can you lure any customers from your competitors? Can you develop new customers who have never purchased baby products before? As you can see, the 10%, objective, can come from a variety of sales strategies.

In order for this section to be successful you must have very specific objectives. There must be no gray areas. The more exact and specific you can be about your objective, the greater probability your strategies will be successful. Some areas of strategies might be:

Regional Strategy. George Bush made a visit to Montana during his re-election campaign. The only problem was, his aids didn't do their homework, and scheduled his visit on the first day of deer hunting season. George Bush or a 10 point buck? A lot of folks missed seeing

George that day. Is your business region specific? No one makes sales calls to accountants in March or April. After the 15th might be OK.

Competitive Strategy. What can you do about the competition? Examine your business resume: Do you have an opportunity or a challenge? If your competition has the advantage, move on to another area. Don't dwell on the things you can't do anything about. Unless your competitors have 100% of the market you still have other strategies.

Pricing Strategy: Can you be priced lower than the competition? It's not a good idea to be the lowest price in your market because people equate price to value. The lower the price the lower the value. You may end up having to defend your lower price much like your higher priced competitor must justify their higher one.

 Wal-Mart has been very successful in the low price arena but mostly on their own brands and some specials. For example, Tide is very close to supermarket pricing in Wal-Mart, as are other name brands.

Tell Them:

Publicity Strategy: Do you know how most people or businesses end up in the paper? In the mid 1980's "Raiders of the Lost Ark" was one of the very first Hollywood blockbuster movies released on home video. At the time, I was working for a video rental chain in San Diego, called Video Library. The local news media came to our main office to do an interview with Barry Rosenblatt, the owner, about the film's release. Why did they come to us? Because we called them and let them know this "news event" was about to happen. We were all over the news in San Diego that week and many customers were under the mistaken impression that we were the only chain that had the movie.

That one bit of publicity brought us untold new customers who had never rented from us in the past but became loyal customers.

As you can see, the use of objectives and strategies can really make or break your business. Remember the two rules: 1. Set clear, concise, specific objectives with a goal and time limit. 2. Describe the strategies to reach those goals in great detail and follow your plan to success.

List the steps you'll take to create your plan and the steps to make it work.

Step One:

Chapter Seven:
Step 6: How To Position
Your Business

What is positioning? How do you position your product so the target market will buy it. Positioning is nothing more than a perception of a product in the mind of your target market. This is where your fortune will be made or lost.

Let me explain it this way. If I were to ask you to name a brand of ketchup, most people would probably say Heinz. If I said soup, most people would say Campbell's. If I said Honda, most people would think automobile. If I said computer brand most people would say IBM. Copier, Xerox. Soft drink, Coke. Fast Food, McDonald's. Etc.

When I say, "Name a brand of soup." To some people the store shelves may pop into the mind. For others it might be a childhood memory of watching mother make tomato soup and grilled cheese sandwiches and picturing the soup can on the counter. For another it might be Andy Worhall's famous painting of the Campbell's soup can.

The result of positioning is what pops into the customer's mind of a product versus the competition. When we mention soup, and you say Campbell's, suppose we go one step further and ask for a soup other than Campbell's. You might say Progresso, or Heinz. Heinz? I thought they made ketchup? So, if Campbell's is number one in America it must be number one all over the world...right? Wrong! If you went to the United Kingdom you would find that Heinz is the number one soup in England. So what's the problem here? Don't the Brits' know good soup when they taste it? No, the two soups are the same here that they are in England but the minds are different.

How about this?

If you went to Japan and told a Japanese person you had just bought a Honda, he would probably ask if it was your first motorcycle. In Japan, Honda is best know as a motorcycle company. Would you buy a Harley-Davidson automobile? Maybe? Would you buy Pennzoil Cake Mix? Betty Crocker Motor Oil? How about an IBM lawnmower? Why not? They're good companies aren't they? The name must mean IBM would make its lawn mowers with the same care and technology as their computers. If you saw the IBM lawnmower side by side with the Lawnboy which would you feel more comfortable buying?

Are you beginning to see how powerful positioning can be? How you position your product can be the key to success or failure for your business. You bought this book because of how it was positioned on the smalltownmarketing.com web page or in some other type of ad or promotion. You felt the unseen information was worth the price and made the investment.

So, if I have a soup company, is there no hope for me because of Campbell's domination of the market? No, and that's the real beauty of positioning.

For this next example, I'm going to defer to a great book on this subject and I suggest you run right out and buy it. It's called "Positioning: The Battle For Your Mind" by Al Ries and Jack Trout (Warner Books ISBN# 0-446-34794-9). It has the best examples of the next point I want to make and that is how to compete with the Campbell's and Heinz's of the world. How this all relates to positioning in small towns will follow. But first, a history lesson.

Who's First?

In their book Trout and Ries ask, "Who was the first person to fly solo across the Atlantic Ocean?" Most of you should say Charles

Lindbergh. Who was the second person to fly solo across the Atlantic Ocean? How quickly we forget the household name of ...Bert Hinkler? Yes, good old Bert Hinkler. He flew the distance in a shorter time than Lindbergh and used less fuel. Who was the second person to walk on the moon? Second tallest mountain in the world? If you're second to your competitors are you are in a deep smelly place? No, and here's why.

Be first where you can

Their book goes on to point out, "Who was the third person to fly solo across the Atlantic Ocean?" If you didn't know the second person how on earth could I assume you would know the third? Well, you do. It was Amelia Earhart. But even better for you, Amelia wasn't remembered as the third person to fly solo across the Atlantic — She was what? Exactly, she was the first *woman* to fly solo across the Atlantic Ocean.

What this means is you can position yourself away from your competition into a category where you have less or no competition. Thanks to Al Ries and Jack Trout for pointing out the obvious.

I positioned my company, smalltownmarketing.com, as a place for businesses in small towns to go for business help instead of just another marketing company on the Internet promising the same old stuff. I searched the Internet extensively for any kind of marketing help for business in small towns and found nothing. That doesn't mean there isn't any, just that I didn't find any. There are no books on Amazon.com or Barnes & Noble.com devoted to small town marketing. This will be the first.

Are we alone?

So for the time being I'm alone. As my success grows, more and more imitators will come along and try to lure market share from me. As that happens, just as with any business, my success will depend how strong my position as the authority on small town marketing is in the minds of those who visit the web site or purchase my marketing books, articles and newsletters.

What makes positioning in a small town so different than in a large metropolitan area? Mostly two things:

1.) In a small town more people know you and may have already formed a perception of you before you even start your business. If this perception is that you don't know the business, you will have a challenge in this area. If you buy a pizza business, and have not been in the restaurant business in town before, people may give you the benefit of the doubt and support your business. Or, they may stay away because you couldn't possibly make a decent pizza because of your inexperience. They don't know that for four years at college you worked in a pizza parlor to support yourself and while there you learned the pizza business and that's why you bought the store in the first place.

2.) Because positioning, by its very nature, is mind control of sorts, once people in your small town perceive you in a certain way, it is an uphill climb to change their minds. Plus in a small town word of mouth spreads rapidly.

If you position your product incorrectly in a large city, you have a large enough customer base to overcome that obstacle. You just reposition the product and continue on. In a small town the customer base is more limited and once the damage is done, it's done. And so are you.

How do major businesses in the your industry position themselves?

Set yourself apart

Let's go back to our baby store. How do baby stores in large cities position themselves? Call some up and ask them. Where and how do they advertise? How do they set themselves apart from their competition? What are your strengths compared to your competitor?

You could position yourself as the baby expert store. Bring in pediatricians for seminars. Rent or sell videos on child rearing. Or maybe you're the place to get those unusual baby things that ordinary stores don't carry. Sort of the Sharper Image® of baby products.

When it comes to positioning most small businesses make two major mistakes;

First, they assume the customer thinks like them, acts like them, and has the same interests and motives. They don't do the research. They advertise on radio stations they listen to instead of the stations the target market is listening to.

Second, they assume the consumer will compare similar products logically and make a decision based strictly on the merits of the product. There is an old axiom. "When emotion and logic come into conflict, emotion always wins." We decide by emotion and use logic to justify our emotional decision. Do yourself a favor and take yourself out of the equation. Rely on facts that your market research has uncovered.

Once again, I can't stress the importance of the business resume in Step One of this marketing plan. Ask yourself every conceivable question about your business and its products. You must know your business and its market inside and out. Your positioning must be right-on in a small town. The smaller the town the more difficult the task and there is virtually no margin for error.

Consider the following. Studies have shown the average number of people who attend a funeral is 250. Your sphere of influence is 250 friends, neighbors, co-workers, and relatives. If you live in a town of 5,000 these people are 5% of the total population. If you have to reposition your products or service, start the process with these people. You need to encourage them to spread the word and neutralize the negative position.

Chapter Eight:
Step 7: What do we say, how do we say it and where do we say it?

In order to develop your advertising and promotion strategies you have a few more questions that need to be answered. There are six areas of business that deal with your product or service. You need to define and decide if you will or won't use them in your advertising.

I'll do the products first, then the message, and how we will deliver it.

1. Tangible or Intangible - Products or Service

Tangible products are those we can see, feel, touch, taste, etc. Intangible products are unseen. For example, insurance or clean carpets, (you can touch the carpets, but you can't touch the fact that they are clean). Intangible products are almost always produced by service businesses. If you have a intangible product your description in your advertising must create a picture in the prospects mind because you don't have a product they can touch. Using insurance again, usually the message is peace of mind that insurance will provide for the family in case of emergency.

Promote Both

Michelin Tires sells a tangible product, the tire, but use infants in their commercials to promote how safe (an intangible) you will feel with their tires on your car.

Who Are You?

Once again you need to return to Step One and Step Two of the marketing plan and look for the strengths that need to be included in your message. Are you going to include pictures or testimonials of the staff, management, or customers in your ads? Should experience be included? Is there anything I, as a customer, need to know about you that will influence my buying decision?

2. What's In A Name?

If you are introducing a new product there's a need to create a brand image. Tide, Xerox, IBM, Apple. All spend tremendous amounts of money on promoting their brand names.

The reason we think of these brands first is due to the constant bombardment of their names by advertising day in and day out. Will we forget them if we don't hear about them? You bet.

Has it been awhile since you thought about Ipana Toothpaste? Bucky Beaver? Most of you have never heard of Ipana at all. It was a major brand name in the fifties. Now sold only in one or two Midwestern states.

Look at your competitors. How have they positioned their brand names? Are you going to be a second or third choice of the customer? Or, are you going to position your name in a different category?

Don't judge a book by its cover

Ever buy a book or magazine based on the cover or the hype and discovered afterwards it was not what you expected? Brand names are certainly important, but so is something else, packaging. The physical look of the product. A box of Tide for example. There is tangible and intangible packaging just like the product or services mentioned on the previous pages. We'll deal with that in just a minute. Let's go back to our box of Tide.

3. How do we compare?

When they package that box of Tide, which will be displayed with their competitors, how they look next to them becomes critical. Color, typestyles and design are what attracts customers to the product. The message on the product causes them to either logically or emotionally evaluate your product and make a purchase. Or they return it to the shelf and buy the competitor's brand.

Intangible Packaging

Probably the best place to see examples of this is in the yellow pages. Here, similar competitors are all displayed together and studies show the bigger the ad, the more response that ad gets. I'll cover the Yellow Pages in more detail later.

Pick a section of the Yellow Pages and study it. The largest ads are usually personal injury attorneys. They are half to full page ads. How do they position themselves? How do they set themselves apart from their competition? What points do they stress?

You don't need complicated logo's, fancy typestyles, or electric colors. Keep it simple but make it effective. If you're not sure of your designs, bring in a group of family members or customers and ask them to evaluate sample ads and packaging ideas. Ask them what they like or don't like about each one. Make a check list of 1 to 10 on several points. "On a scale of 1 to

10 what do you think of ...?" Don't ask which one they like best. You'll just put undo pressure on them that there may be a wrong answer hidden somewhere. Make it as easy as possible to be honest and anonymous. They will provide more information if they are unknown.

4. Pricing

Are you going to publish pricing in your advertising? In sales and promotions, maybe yes. As a general rule, probably not. Why? When there is only price with no described benefit or perceived value customers become skeptical. When I worked at Circuit City, in their video department, we had a sale that started every Thursday and ended every Sunday. We always had a low priced sale on TV's, VCR's, camcorder's, etc. Customers would come in and ask to see the sale item. The first question was usually something like, "What's wrong with it?" or "How come it's so cheap?"

Price has to be attached to real benefits before it becomes a consideration. Every feature of a product must have a corresponding benefit to the customer. If the feature is not a benefit, it is useless information.

The more features to benefits the product has the less consideration about the price and the more valuable the product is in the eyes of the consumer.

5. How do we get it to the customer?

How do you get your product to the customer? And how do you say that in your ad? Does the customer pick it up? Does it have to be shipped? Mailed? Delivered? FedEx? How does your distribution stack up against your competitors? Are you faster? Slower? Cheaper? More Expensive?

All customers expect a timely delivery of the product. In the furniture business, I would much rather sell something in stock rather than special order. The sale is completed almost immediately. The delivery is scheduled and the customer has seen what they are going to receive. With special orders there is time for the customer to find something they like better and cancel the sale. If they already have the merchandise there is less chance of a cancellation.

Effective distribution is a huge customer sales plus. The more effective you are at delivering the product the better your business will be.

6. Who contacts the customer?

Are you going to use direct selling in your business? In other words, does a commission salesperson physically sell the product to a customer one-on-one. Or, do they order it by catalog or buy off the shelf at your location? Is it a self service operation? What selling aids do your salespeople need? Catalogs, price lists, computer, order forms, etc. What are the costs related to these activities?

Many car dealers tout in their ads the length of time some of their salespeople have been with them. For many people, length of service is a positive and feel they will be better taken care of by someone experienced.

If you are an Internet business, you don't have much of a track record because the Internet is still in its infancy. So the customer may be willing to forgive your inexperience because the majority of Internet businesses are inexperienced.

Some people dislike salespeople. They would rather look on their own. However, if you have a crack sales staff, talk about them. In many cases the crack sales staff will be you.

What are your sales strategies? Remember the Victor Business Machines story? Seventy-five cold calls, 20 machine placements, 5 sales. That was their sales strategy. Do your salespeople need to be certified or licensed? Will they need special training at schools or seminars? Reaching the customer is the focus. If we can't sell the customer, the business is destined for failure.

Rule of Two's

Fred E. Hahn and Kenneth G. Mangun in their book, "Do-It-Yourself Adverting and Promotion" (John Wiley &Sons, Inc. ISBN #0-471-15442-3) define the "Rule of Two's and the "Rule of Three."

The Rule of Two's simply means, "See an ad once, it's a test; see it twice it's a success." Look at where you're competitors ads are running. If they start to advertise anywhere on a consistent basis, they must be getting some ROI (Return On Investment) from the ads.

What are your competitors doing. Quick point. Don't become obsessed with your competitor's message. You don't want your competitors to always dictate how and where you advertise, but there are some things to look for.

Monitor your competitor's ads and look for a response request. Is there a "Call To Action?"

"Half -Off!" This does not qualify as a call to action. "Bring this coupon and get Half-Off all week-end" is designed to bring customers to your competitor's location. If there is no Call To Action how can your competitor know the ads' drawing power?

Key your ads. (I'll cover this in detail later.) But in a nutshell, keying your ads means that the "call to action" message in that ad will let you know which media the ad came from. It might be a code number printed in a corner of a coupon. Or an "Ask for John", or ask for extension 200 as a phone call. Using this method you can evaluate the power of the ad and decide if it's worth running again. Don't waste advertising money by running ads that don't pull customers. If you're running a new series of ads, make sure you allow enough time between ads to evaluate the effectiveness of the campaign.

The Rule of Three

According to Hahn and Mangun, the "Rule of Three" says, An ad message must appear three times in media that is seen or read by the same audience before you can expect it to be noticed once. Studies show that it takes 9 impressions of an ad before people have the confidence to try your business. Applying their "rule of three", you will need to run your ad 27 times before it becomes effective. This type of advertising is useful in name recognition advertising. It also explains why advertising doesn't always work immediately. And why you need to pay attention to the "rule of two."

Not sure where to advertise?

The public and university libraries have S.R.D.S. (Standard Rate and Data Service) Directories. They are guides to the full range of options on advertising to a specific audience or in a particular field. They contain detailed information, field by field, on nearly every medium that accepts advertising. For more information, check their web site at http://www.SRDS.com or write them at S.R.D.S., 1700 Higgins, Des Plains, NY 60018, or call (847) 375-5000.

Next, The Message: Who to and How?

Have you ever wondered, "What makes a great ad?" John McWade, is the founder of PageLab, Sacramento, CA (916-443-4890), the first desktop publishing studio. Here are some of the things he looks for:

1.) We all like surprises. Can you state an ordinary message in an unusual way. Not comedy, but differently. Commercials done this way are the ones we talk about at work the next day.

2.) Keep it simple. Don't let the design overpower the message. The idea is the most important part of the message.

3.) Get me involved. Shock me, make me mad, make me happy, make me cry, but don't bore me and leave me cold.

4.) Make me curious. Isn't the real purpose of an ad to make me want more information? Grab my attention and hold it.

5.) They command answers. They demand that you respond to the ad. They are like an unanswered question that must be resolved.

6.) Draw your own conclusion. Isn't the strongest conclusion the one we draw ourselves? An ad that brings me to a conclusion is powerful indeed.

7.) The headline and the image tell the story. The headline should never tell you what is in the picture. Only what you don't see. The headline and picture create the story.

8.) They never brag. I keep coming back to Yellowstone Harley-Davidson in Belgrade, Montana. Their billboard at the edge of town proclaims, "The largest Harley-Davidson Dealer in Belgrade!" A town of 4,000 people. They are also the only dealer in over a hundred miles. Just a fact, not a brag.

9.) Great ads are always well executed. They have good design that doesn't overpower the message. They have sharp photos, good typefaces, etc.

10. They Sell. The most important function of any ad. What good is an ad that wins award after award if it doesn't sell?

Apply the rules

We know our target group and we know our product. Next, we've got to get our message out to our target group at a cost that's within our budget. Let's look at the five most popular methods of getting the message out.

1.) Promotion: First order of business, Goals. As with everything else I talk about in this book, you have to know what you want your promotion to accomplish. You can't begin to decide how to promote if you don't have an expectation of the end result. Perhaps you expect to bring X number of customers into the business the first week, month or X number of phone inquiries. If you know the goal, it's much easier to create the promotion.

Small Town Advantage

Promotion is one area where being in a small town is an advantage to business. You are reaching a small area and even though you have competition you have less than in most large cities. You should have a certain amount of money allocated to advertising and promotion in your business plan. Your business may live or die depending on how you spend this money.

Getting Started

To promote your business there are a host of things you can do. Coupons, contests and sweepstakes, sales, or rebates all should increase traffic to your business. Which one or combination depends on the goals you set. Which will accomplish the goal most economically?

New Business?

If you are a new business, the first item of business is the promotion of a Grand Opening. (I think every retail business should have an annual Grand Opening.) New people move to town, and they may not know about your business. Established residents will begin to look forward to your yearly event and promote it for you by word-of-mouth.

Dealing with the media

Contact the local media about your Grand Opening three to six months before your opening and see what options are available to you.

Is your store opening a news event? Have you made your business unique in some way? TV stations may want to cover your opening or at least do a story about the business. Radio stations love to do live remote broadcasts at new businesses, but are usually are not free. Newspapers featuring an article on your new business is worth much more than any grand opening ad. Many papers have a "People In Business" section where you can put a small announcement about your business. It's not always easy to reach these media people and convince them you are genuine news and not trying to con them into doing some free publicity.

Newspapers, TV magazines and radio usually have reduced rates for new or first time advertisers. You may need to sign up for a certain amount of ads or spots to get the reduced rates.

Mailing Lists?

One of the least expensive ways to get your message out in a small town is direct mail. The first order of business is to create a mailing list. You could purchase a list from a mailing list broker but this is sometimes prohibitive for a small town because you need to purchase a minimum number of names.

I did a promotion for a spa dealer in Bozeman. One of the criteria we needed was an annual income of $40,000. The listing company had a 3,000 name minimum at a price of $35.00 per thousand. To get enough names with that income we had to expand the list to include five other counties. Because of servicing costs the spa company would only sell in two of those counties. The cost was only a little over $100.00 but had to purchase a lot of names they'd never use, just to get the names in Bozeman and the surrounding area. It was faster than creating a specialized list which I'll cover next.

Check at the chamber

Pick up a membership directory from your local chamber of commerce and create a mailing list. Sit down and hand type the mailing labels. Many chambers have a list in mailing label form they sell. If you can't afford that, make your own from the directory. You can also get mailing lists from the post office. You can buy specific postal routes for specific neighborhoods. You can send postcards (.20¢ each = $20.00 per 100 Cards) or letters/ brochures (.33¢ each = $33.00 per 100) for specific neighborhoods announcing your Grand Opening. What about bulk mail? Isn't it less expensive than a first class mailing?

Yes, it is, but there are some strong disadvantages to bulk mail. The first disadvantage is bulk mail is not always delivered in a timely manner by the post office. It is included with other mail as volume permits. It could possibly be delivered after your grand opening is over. Second disadvantage - customers look through the mail over the waste basket and many bulk mail pieces go directly into the trash without even being opened. That's why I like postcards. They are 1¢ more than bulk mail rates, they are delivered with first class mail. If you include "Address Correction Requested" under the return address the post office will update your mailing list free, and finally they are almost always read by more than just the person they are addressed to.

Key Your Postcards (Give customers a reason to keep the card and bring it in)

As a key to your mailings, ask your customers to bring the postcard as an entry to a sweepstakes or drawing for free gifts. Keep the mailing lists and mail to these people two to three times over the next six to eight months. Why? Because you need to develop a "name recognition" with your customers.

Name Recognition

You are a new business. Customers need to learn your name and associate it with your business. If they only see your name once how are they going to remember your business? How many people have you met one time and remembered their name? It's the same with your business. The customer needs to hear your name over and over to reinforce the name in their minds.

Established Business?

If you are an established business, you have established customers. Build your business on them. Have a special sale or event for these customers who have supported you over the years. Show them that you appreciate their support and they will promote your business for you. A referral from an existing customer is the most powerful type of business contact.

"John Smith sent me in." is much more powerful than, "I saw your ad in the Daily Journal." Remember, your good name is what your business survives on in the long haul. It's impossible to place a value on this kind of promotion.

2.) What's your advertising message?: When we talk about advertising we are talking about two basic concepts. Advertising informs and/or persuades your customers to do something. If you're a new business, you will use both concepts. Inform (name recognition/product existence) and persuade the customer to consider the purchase of your product or service.

Advertising Objectives:

Just like your sales objectives, you need to set advertising goals and objectives. What will your advertising accomplish? How long will it take? What will it cost? What type of strategy are you going to use?

Benefit

What benefit will the target market receive from your product? What problem will be solved?

What assurance can you offer that the risk of trying or using your product will be minimal?

Oh, What A Feeling!

What is the feeling your advertising conveys to the customer? For example: If I'm selling used cars I may do a lot of shouting and exclamation of our great weekend car sale. If I'm from a funeral parlor, I'm going to have a much more subdued and refined delivery. I'm not going to yell and scream about our weekend casket sale.

How to execute

If you're spearheading the advertising yourself, there are some things you need to be aware of.

1.) How your logos and business name are presented in the ad. All your ads, brochures, TV spots, radio should maintain a certain "family resemblance."

2.) Are legal disclaimers required and how are they shown in the ad?

3.) What product lines are included? Does the customer need to be educated about your line?

4.) Store name, phone, address etc? Where do they appear? How large?

5.) Colors? Typefaces? Ad placement location?

6.) Co-Op advertising? How are other companies logos used? What hoops do you have to jump through to get your co-op money?

Your advertising goals and target market information will make it easier to decide on the type of media to use to get your message out.

How to choose the best media mix for your message.

In a small town you will probably start with the local media choices that are available to you. This can be both good and bad. New businesses are tempted to advertise in all available media. Everything from the local newspaper to a spot in the back of the high school yearbook. You want to get the message out but your advertising budget is probably limited and you must be smart in how and where your message is presented. As your company grows, more advertising options will be open to you. For now lets concentrate on the basics. As I mentioned above, you want your advertising to have a "family resemblance." In other words, your newspaper ads should "resemble" your brochure, and other print ads. Unseen ads like radio should send the same message as the newspaper and brochure. Each time an ad is exposed to one of your customers it is constantly reinforced by another ad in another medium. The customer starts to feel comfortable with the message. Let's talk about four points you must deal with in choosing where to put your messages.

1.) You want to be noticed by the largest segment of your target market. From the target market section of the plan you should have a fairly accurate idea by now of who your target market is. The questions then become: What percentage listen to what radio stations, read what newspapers, etc?

2.) Use your advertising dollars in the most economical way. For example, you might use TV as a short time media to promote your Grand Opening. But the cost of TV might be prohibitive for your day-to-day advertising.

3.) You may have primary and secondary target markets. You need to be sure that the media you choose will reach the key groups within your total target market.

4.) When using different media, you must stay on top of your advertising. Be sure there is consistency of image about your business. Make sure your spots are running when they're supposed to and with the correct message. Running a sale ad *after* the sale is over is a poor use of your advertising budget.

Frequency, Reach, Impressions, Rating Points, What does all that mean?

Let's look at each one.

1.) Frequency - This term refers to the number of times one specific customer actually sees your ad. It may play 100 times, but if only one person sees it one time, your frequency is 1.

Use frequency if you are trying to:

A. Capture the same market as your competitor (McDonalds vs. Burger King)
B. When you want customers to order the product then and there.
C. Customer must act within a certain time period.
There's not a lot of difference between you and your competitors.

2.) Reach - This term is often presented with frequency because they are "first cousins". Reach is the total number of households exposed to your message over a specific period of time. The best example of Reach I can think of is The Super Bowl. The frequency is once a year and the reach is a good portion of the planet. Remember, when you run a newspaper ad, it reaches a lot of people. Many of those people are not your customers and never will be. So Reach is important to examine.

Go for greater reach:

A. Introducing a new product to a broad mass market and want as many as possible to know about it. The greatest commercial ever made (according to Advertising Age®) ran only one time — during the 1984 Super Bowl. It was the ad announcing the new Macintosh® computer from Apple Computer®.
B. If the message is so good customers will react immediately.
C. When the product is newsworthy (Cancer Cure), and will demand attention all by itself.

3.) Impressions - The total of all exposures of the ad to all people that see the ad. For example, a newspaper has 10,000 readers per day. Of those, 8,000 read the sports page on a regular basis. If you run an ad in the sports pages every day for thirty days that's 240,000 impressions. 30 ads X 8,000 readers.

4.) Ratings Point - These are measures of selected TV and radio audiences used to equalize in the customers eyes how one program relates to another and they base their advertising pricing on these numbers.

Media Objectives

If I were to write a media objective for my radio ads it might look like this:

The ad should reach 75% of my primary target market an average of 5 times and 40% of my secondary market at least three times in the first 30 days. So, if I've defined my target market correctly and place my ads with the correct media I should expect favorable results.

In large cities, advertising agencies would take care of all this for you as part of their services. But in a small town you'll have to do it yourself. Let's look at how you do it.

Selecting the right media.

Now that you have your goals and objectives of what you want your advertising to accomplish, it's time to pick the advertising media(s) to present your message.

1.) List and review as many sources and possibilities as you can for reaching your target audience.

Don't be concerned about cost at this point. You want a list of as many ways to reach your market as possible. For example, if I wanted to reach senior citizens, I might want to look at

Senior Golf Journal and Modern Maturity.
Many seniors own motor homes so maybe
Motor Home Magazine would be a
consideration. Many seniors are housebound, so
the local edition of the TV Guide or the TV
listings in the newspapers should be considered.
List as many as you can and don't limit your
options. One of the best ways of finding out
where your customers get their information is to
ask them. Ask how they heard about you. Most
people enjoy talking about themselves - so ask.
They don't need to know you're doing research.
Have them fill out a Satisfaction Report Card.
Warranty cards are another good source of
information.

Radio, TV, magazines and newspapers will each
have demographic profiles of their readers,
listeners and viewers. Start by matching up the
profiles of the various media with the profiles
from the target market section of your
marketing plan. The library will have listings
and addresses of magazines that may be popular
in your area. In Bozeman we have Montana
Magazine, many Bozeman businesses advertise
there.

Start with the biggest media first and narrow
your choices as you go. I mentioned above that
TV might be possible for a grand opening or big

sale, but not day-to-day. The same with newspapers. The ads might be bigger for a huge sale but smaller for name recognition.

2.) Get a media kit from each potential media and study it.

A media kit will have all the necessary information about the readership of a newspaper or magazine, or the viewership or listenership of radio or TV. It should contain the demographics needed for your customer demographics. Billboard companies should also provide you with pricing, availability and location of available billboards.

3.) Form a relationship with your advertising representative.

These are the people who have the greatest influence as to where your ad may be placed or when it's aired. In small towns the sales rep may also be the general manager at the radio or TV station. They can help you — make friends with them and let them know you appreciate their efforts. Although most are paid on commission and are always trying to sell you more than you may need; they can often provide special deals and promo's that may cut costs.

4.) Choose a combination of media with the right impact

Remember, your goal is to pick the least expensive advertising with the "biggest bang for the buck." This refers to your whole package, not each individual part. A radio and newspaper ad may cost less and reach a bigger segment of your target market for a longer time than a one time TV spot on prime time. Make your advertising pay.

5.) How time-sensitive is your advertising?

If you are going to run a magazine ad, it may take three to six months before your ad will see the customer. This is fine if you know in advance what you're going to run and for how long. Remember, magazines tend to hang around for weeks, months, even years in some doctors' offices. If you need a quick result then magazines are not your best bet. For short time ads, use radio, newspapers, and TV. In most small towns it will be radio and newspapers.

6.) Frequency and Exposure

We defined frequency as the number of times a specific customer sees your ad. It has also been defined as the total number of times an ad is run in a specific media. Going back to our comparison of time. Ads in the daily newspaper often end up on the bottom of the bird cage before the day is done. They are seen once and the paper is in the trash. Your ad is gone. Conversely, people tend to hang on to magazines that are devoted to their interests and the ad stays around a little longer. Using this argument, a daily newspaper would require more frequency than a monthly magazine.

Be *consistent* in your advertising. Placing an ad three times in the same media in the same place has a much better chance of being noticed than the same ad once or twice. Six to nine times and things can really get exciting. I can't stress this point enough. There is no "instant gratification" in marketing or advertising. It takes time to sow the seeds and reap the harvest. Put your message out there consistently and get it working. If you invest in the stock market, there is always a chance the market will go down and you'll lose money. If the market goes up you make money. Advertising and marketing are no different. They are investments. They are not too expensive. They aren't an expense at all (although it may seem that way when you sign the checks for it.) Advertising, if done correctly, is an investment in your business and your future.

Many marketing books will tell you that running an ad too many times in the same place will bore people and the message loses impact. I disagree with this thinking, because as a society we are not a stagnant pond, we are a whitewater rapid. We are constantly on the move and we dismiss many of the thousands of daily messages that bombard us. We move from place to place more than any country on earth. Bozeman changes its entire population every 10 to 12 years mostly because of the winters. People were predicting Montana population would reach 1 million people by 1975. We're still at 800,000 for the state.

Several years ago my wife and I attended an automobile show in San Diego. We both fell in love with the Mazda RX-7 but we could not recall seeing any of these cars in the San Diego area. However, we were amazed on the drive home they seemed to be everywhere. We must have seen 15 to 20 on our drive back to the house. "Why hadn't we seen these cars before?" They were obviously there.

We decided that all cars, except for those in our immediate path, were blocked out of our minds as unimportant in our lives at that time. As long as your ad is producing customers let it run. I don't care how boring it is to you and your employees, it's new to a lot of people who will be seeing it for the first time. If it is not working after a reasonable period of time, then it may be time for a new campaign. Campbell's Soup has been using "Mmm-mm Good!" for a long time and Budweiser has been the "King of Beers" for a long time.

7.) Demographic numbers - How do I know they're right?

Radio, TV and newspapers all fall under forms of self industry regulation. They have taken it upon themselves to do their own policing and keep their industry clean. They use independent outside sources to conduct audits on various industries.

For TV, it's the Arbitron Company and A. C. Nielson Company that audit viewers and report who's watching what, and when. Magazines use Business/Professional Advertising Association (BPAA). Newspapers use the Audit Bureau of Circulation (ABC).

What should advertising cost?

Advertising costs are going to vary depending on where you live and the competition in your markets. Here are some things to consider as you look at the pricing in your home town.

If the price of *producing* the ad is more than the actual *cost* of running the ad, something is wrong. Either you have a great ad and aren't running it enough or you're running it in the wrong place.

Another way sales reps look at the cost of advertising is the good old price per 1,000 listeners/viewers to a particular show or spot in the program lineup.

Your interest should be in the cost per *customer* of your advertising. If I buy 3 spots for $10.00 each ($30.00) and that produces one customer that spends $20.00, what just happened. Your advertising has suddenly become an expense, not an investment. You want to reach people but if your advertising is producing non-paying customers it's useless.

Reduce advertising costs

So, can you reduce the cost of advertising until the buyers start coming? Yes, here are a couple of ways:

Co-op advertising -

Companies will pick up part of your advertising tab if you include their logo and product in the ads. For example, a paint store can run an ad featuring Benjamin-Moore Paints and the paint company will pay for a portion of the ad. Caution: Submit the ad to the co-op company for approval first. If you don't use their logo and copy within their guidelines they will disqualify you for the funds. Also, be patient in waiting for the co-op money. It is almost always paid after the ad has run. Sometimes weeks, even months may go by before the check arrives. One way to speed up payment is by offering to accept payment in the form of a discount on your next order.

Joint and Cross Promotions -

Can you join forces with other companies and combine your advertising dollars? Video stores and pizza parlors? Our paint company with a paintbrush company?

Combining products will sometimes make both products stronger together than they were apart. Advertising them together is more economical than separately.

Which media is best for you?

Next, we'll look at the different kinds of media available to you and examine the strengths and weaknesses of each.

Newspapers

Newspapers are mostly standard size (like the New York Times) or Tabloid size (like the National Inquirer). They are daily, biweekly, weekly, and in rare cases monthly. Some strengths of newspapers are:

Speed: ads can be produced quickly and influence your customer immediately.

Local markets: Many small towns have some form of daily newspaper. They are one of the best ways to reach local and small markets.

Sections: If you're a stock broker you can be in the business section, shoe store the family section, grocery store the food section. Be where your customers are!

Budget: Newspapers have ads in a variety of sizes that can fit most small business budgets.

Some weaknesses of newspapers are:

Short life: Sometimes they're on the bottom of the bird cage by 10:00 am. Even worse, if someone misses the paper one day, they miss your ad.

Ad placement: Where's a good place to have your ad? How about next to the daily horoscope. Even people who don't believe in it check it often. But, even if you request that location, you may not get it. Your ad can be lost among others on the page.

Demonstration: If your product's story is best told visually, newspapers have some real restrictions. Even photos require a good sized ad to make them visible. TV might be a better buy here.

It's news print: The quality of newspapers compared to magazines leaves a lot to be desired. The paper used is called news print paper. To produce that kind of quality, on good paper, the daily paper would cost upwards of $5.00 or more per day.

Dealing with Print Ads

If you have the computer hardware, you may want to create your *own* print ads. If you do, here are the things I do when I create an ad:

First, start with all the elements that must be in the ad. These include: your logo, address, phone number and any other items that mention name recognition. After I have those in place, I can then see how much space I have left for the message.

Next, I want to combine a strong visual with a very brief, but powerful, message about the business. The purpose of the ad is not to make the sale, the purpose to the ad is to entice the customer to call or come by or write to you. When that happens the sales process can begin.

I also want to stay about 1/8th to 3/8ths inch away from the edge of the ad. Why? Because I know my ad may be clumped in with a lot of other ads and this little area of white space will help my ad stand out from the others. Don't feel you have to fill every available inch of space with your message. The same is true in brochures and business cards. These items aren't intended to make the sale. Their purpose is to alert the customer to your business and educate them about a need they might not know they had.

Color?

If you can afford color, use it! If you can't afford it, do the best you can for now. Four color ads get a much higher response than ads with no color at all. One or two colors are always better than just black and white. At least price color when talking with your media reps.

Caution: Sometimes color will only be used in certain sections and on certain pages of the paper...be careful of placement of your color ad.

Size?

Make your ad as large as you can afford. Here is where advertising and marketing is an investment. If you go with the size ad you can afford now you are safe. Advertising is not a risk for you. But if you go with a larger ad you should receive more calls and more business and the ad pays for itself. I would suggest you go with an ad one step above what is comfortable for you.

Newspaper Ad Position:

To avoid being unhappy with the placement of your ad, make sure you will be in the correct section of the paper. Economy, sports, editorial, etc. In some cases you may be able to pay extra for special placement of your ad. The best places to be in the paper, best to worst, are:

1.) page 2 or 3 of the news section,
2.) the back page of any section (except classified ads),
3.) the first three pages of any section (except classifieds),
4.) pages 4 and up in the news section

Better placement and value:

Many local businesses like the weekly TV section. In San Diego, this section was filled with construction people, advertising home remodeling and room additions. The TV section stays around all week while the rest of the paper ended up in the trash.

Regional Sections:

In Montana, the Billings Gazette is available in most cities in the state. The Gazette often includes a regional section in their paper for Bozeman, Butte, Missoula, and other cities around the state. The regional sections may be available at a lower price but mostly contain club and organization news of little interest to most readers. You may not get the biggest bang for your buck in this section. Contact businesses that are currently in these sections and see what kind of responses they are experiencing.

Special Events Sections:

Many newspapers have special events sections during the year. Car shows, boat shows, bridal fairs, home improvement, etc. Before placing ads in these get a copy of the previous years edition. If it's mostly ads, with some stock articles as filler between those ads, it's probably not a good investment of your advertising dollar.

Advertising Inserts:

Take an 8 1/2 x 11 piece of paper, create an advertising piece and have the newspaper include it as an insert with the paper. It's dramatically cheaper than an ad of the same size in the paper and can be color, or at least on colored paper. You can also have it included in certain newspaper routes. If you are selling a high ticket item you may want the flyer to only go to the more affluent parts of town.

Key your ads:

How will you know if your ads are bringing any customers to your business? Put something in the ad that will let you know where they saw the ad. The most common key is a coupon. If you have coupons in lots of places, put a code of some kind on each to show where it came from. If it's in the Daily Gazette in the first week of June, your code might be DG1/6. If you get a lot of coupons you'll know that medium is reaching your target audience. If you don't, consider changing the ad or going with another medium.

Other keys: Call and ask for Jim; Ask about our "Special Offer"; Ask for your free brochure about "your product".

Newspaper Cost:

Newspapers base their pricing on circulation numbers (how many people subscribe), size of ad, color, and any kind of special placement of your ad. Frequent advertisers get better pricing than once-in-while advertisers.

Final thoughts on newspapers:

Not every small town has a great paper. But, even with their weaknesses, the newspaper is a great buy in most small markets and small towns for most companies.

Magazines:

Almost every kind of business has some kind of magazine devoted to it. It never ceases to amaze me, as I travel around and meet businesspeople, the variety of trade magazines that are available to small business. You can take almost any trade name or industry and add the word "Today" on the end and you'll have a trade magazine. Concrete Today, Mobile Homes Today, Bird Watching Today, the list goes on and on.

Magazines are classified by content, geography (Montana Magazine), and whether they are business to business, special interest or for general public consumption.

Magazine Strengths:

Long life: As I mentioned above, some magazines stay in doctors offices' for years. Your ad stays there with it. Great for name recognition.

Narrow Target Market: If you have a narrow target market, this is an excellent way to reach those people. They are seeking out this type of information and will pay more attention to the ads than a casual reader of "People Magazine" would.

Versatile: Have you ever scratched off a spot in a magazine to sample a perfume fragrance? Ever seen a fold-out in a magazine? Special inks? Heavy paper? There are a lot things magazines can do other media can't.

Credibility: Remember Good Housekeeping Magazine? Every company wanted the Good Housekeeping Seal Of Approval on their products. Some magazines have excellent reputations and an ad transfers that reputation to your company in the eyes of some loyal readers.

Magazine Weaknesses:

Long lead time: It takes a while to get your ad to the magazine. To advertise my website for Christmas, I'll need to have the copy in by the end of June. I'm not sure what the website will look like in December. Certainly different than it looks now.

High Cost: Many national magazines are price prohibitive. A national ad in "People" can exceed $100,000 per page. Many national magazines produce regional issues and those rates, though still high, are more reasonable for small business. TV Guide is a good example of a magazine that offers regional advertising.

Size and Color: Magazines offer great color (for a price, usually high) that other media can't touch.

Limited Space: Magazine editors don't want the ads to overpower the content of the magazine. Except in the case of "People" special issues where the ad pages often outnumber the content 2 to 1. It's easy for your ad to be lost in popular magazines because they are crowded.

Low frequency: Monthly magazines are 12 per year. You may need to have other advertising in place to reinforce your magazine advertising.

Magazine Ad Placement:

The best places to put your ad in a magazine, best to worst, are:

1.) The inside front cover,
2.) the back cover,
3.) the first few pages of the magazine,
4.) directly across from the cover story or the feature story,
5.) the inside back cover,
6.) the first 25% of the magazine,
7.) the next 50% of the magazine,
8.) the last 25% of the magazine.

These may vary from magazine to magazine. One way to find out what's successful in magazines is to look at back issues. If the same companies keep showing up in the same spot month after month, you know it must be working.

Some final thoughts on magazines

If you can afford magazine advertising, especially in color, it can be very rewarding for your business. It stays around a long time as opposed to other media and has the power to be the most professional and eye catching presentation.

Radio:

Radio has three categories: Local, used by most advertisers in small towns, for 30 or 60 second commercials; Spot, ads that are sold to national advertisers for local markets; and network which reach all stations in the national network.

Radio Strengths:

Reach and Influence: Radio reaches a lot of people quickly and radio reaches a larger audience than any other media. Homes often have multiple radios. Car radios, portable radios, and radios in the workplace expose your business to countless thousands every day.

Production Costs: Radio commercials are less expensive to create than TV commercials. You can create a "word picture" on radio that would be cost prohibitive to produce on TV.

Cost per thousand: (Review page 111, Cost per customer) Radio is priced at cost per thousand listeners. It's one of the lowest cost per thousand available.

Formats: Radio station formats include talk, rock, new age, rap, country and contemporary to name just a few. Each station has its own distinctive audience. Match your target to the right station and radio is a great advertising buy.

Anything you can imagine: Several years ago Stan Freeburg made a commercial touting the power of your imagination in the use of radio. In the commercial, Lake Michigan had been drained and filled with hot chocolate and a plane towing a giant marshmallow was flying over to drop it. Can you picture this in your mind? With today's computer enhancements this would be easy to create on TV but the cost would be astronomical. On radio just paint a "word picture" and you're done.

Radio Weaknesses:

Short Shelf Life: Unlike newspapers and magazines, once the commercial airs it's gone forever. It's not around to refer to later. Radio requires lots of spots on different stations to reach the majority of the listeners.

Visuals: If your customer needs to see your product to appreciate it then radio is very limited. You could use radio to direct the customer to a product demonstration.

Listener loyalty: Radio is a very competitive market. In Bozeman we have several stations for all of Gallatin Valley. Most listeners are very loyal to their stations. To reach the majority of listeners it may be necessary to advertise on several stations instead of just one or two.

Broad Range: If you're selling to business owners, for example, your message will be largely ignored by all non-business listeners.

Background: Many listeners have the radio on at work at a low volume for background music and never hear your commercial.

Message content:

A radio message usually has three major components:

1.) An attention getting introduction. Distinctive music, sound effects or "jingles" can accomplish this.

2.) The main message of the commercial which should create interest in the product or service; and

3.) A call to action. "Come down today." "Buy Now!" Etc.

Check em' out:

Do a little homework. Get the listings of radio stations in your area and start listening to them.

Pay particular attention to who is advertising on what station. Does the "tone" of the commercial fit the station? You might not find a commercial for the upcoming symphony season on a rap station.

Target Market Match:

When picking a station you will need to match your target market to the station. Here are some ways to do it:

From your target market profile, when is your target market most likely to be listening? Do they go to work early? Do they work nights? Weekends?

Match your product to the stations programming. For examples, Cadillacs and investment shows, lawnmowers and garden shows.

Radio Ad Placement:

The best placement for radio ads (best to worst) are:

Morning and evening drive time: On the way to and from work, you have a captive audience sitting in traffic with the radio as a diversion.

Weekend mornings: Sit down with a cup of coffee and the paper, and flip on the radio to catch up on the weather, news, etc.

Work hours for certain kinds of stations: Jazz, easy listening, and classical stations are used as background music in many businesses. Although this is not the ideal place to put your ads they still receive exposure in a lot of retail establishments.

Specialty Shows: Tie your product into a theme show. For instance, your camping equipment to an outdoor show or your car painting business to a car show.

Guidelines for Radio:

Here are a few pointers to keep in mind when using radio.

1.) Running several commercials per day over a period of weeks is better than spacing them out over a period of months.

2.) If you're in a group of commercials at the top of the hour, ask to be the first commercial in the chain. Listeners will still be focused on the show and you can keep their attention.

3.) Ask to have your commercials placed in the middle of the show rather than the beginning or the end. Once the program ends the listener may turn off the radio and go do something else.

4.) If one of the announcers is well respected in the community you might want to ask for them to read your commercial live. This practice continues the "tone" of the program and is more likely to keep the listeners attention.

Final thoughts on radio:

All things considered, for the small or new business, radio is the best value available for reaching large numbers of customers quickly and easily. Radio spots can be produced and on the air in a matter of hours as opposed to days and sometimes months for other media.

Television:

Most small towns don't have local television stations. However, I'm going to cover this area because the time may come when your business reaches a size that you'll want to advertise on one of the stations that reaches your community. And the television industry is the most powerful means of reaching mass numbers of customers quickly.

Television has gone through several transitions in the past 10 years or so. For years, network television, had a lock on all TV viewers. ABC,

NBC, and CBS did virtually all of the advertising in the nation. In the late 1960's cable started to emerge and siphon off some of the network viewers. Cable movie channels began to offer what every TV viewer dreamed of...an uninterrupted show with no commercials.

Then came specialty channels that did carry advertising; ESPN®, Weather Channel®, Discovery®, Home Shopping Network®, The Sci-Fi Channel®, The Comedy Channel® and yes, even the Golf Channel®. With cable the business advertiser could now pick and choose which channels to be on and when. Package deals became available. An advertiser could be on several channels each day for less than a single spot on a network prime-time show. In radio, as I mentioned, people tend to stay with one station most of the time. In TV, people "channel surf" through the selections until they find something that interests them.

What else is coming in the future? How about High-Definition TV? Better picture, better sound and the Internet right on your TV screen. You will be watching a show, see someone in a suit or dress you like, choose it, and after the show you can go to a "cyberstore" on your TV and get the price, sizes and order the article right off the TV with a credit card. Men would love to shop this way but I think the jury's still out on the women.

Strengths of TV:

It reaches everyone: Not everyone reads the paper, or magazines, but almost everyone watches TV some portion of every day, either for entertainment or news or just relaxation. TV can reach and influence better than any other advertising medium.

It's visual: If your product requires some kind of demonstration or instruction, TV is your medium. Could magazines and newspapers have sold the Hula Hoop as well as TV did?

Uses both sight and sound: Radio is hearing, newspapers and magazines are seeing. TV combines not only sight and sound but, depending on your imagination, taste and smell. Ever see a food ad and your mouth starts watering? You can almost smell the hot rolls or pie.

Using Actors: In national ads, people like Gene Hackman, Ed McMahon and others make a good living as spokespersons for certain products. Advertisers feel that we perceive these people as honest and sincere and we'll be more comfortable buying the product from them. Go in the store and tell them Ed sent you. In a small town you probably aren't going to get Gene Hackman to do the commercials for your store or service but, there are local folks that have celebrity status on a local level. Radio DJ's are the most well known and if they are credible, use them if you can.

Brand Identity: If you are trying to establish your logo or package design, TV is very powerful. You can see the product in use, and see the colors of the package.

Weaknesses of TV

Cost: Even in small markets, TV is expensive. Production costs, time, locations, ideas, re-shoots all add to the expense. One way to save money is to use national ads that have already been made at corporate expense and add your name (called a "tag" or "tag line") and address at the end of the commercial. If you're a paint store, maybe Dutch Boy® has taped commercials you can use and they will pick up part of the cost as co-op advertising.

Here today and gone today: Like radio, once the message is done, it's gone.. Newspapers and magazines keep your ad around but your commercial is gone and the next message is on the way. However, with VCR's it can be seen again when the tape is replayed and can be passed along to others.

Reinforce Your Message: Due to the thousands of messages our brain receives every day, TV spots must be seen often to be effective.

Successful TV Commercials

Have you ever seen an ad in a magazine that looked just like a scene from the TV ad for the same product? A good test of a TV ad is; could you take a single frame from your TV ad and make a magazine ad from it? If you can then the image is successfully telling the story.

All good movies have a beginning, a middle and an end. It's the same with TV. Get the viewers attention, tell the story, reaffirm the message and call for some kind of action.

Placing TV advertising:

Chances are you will be placing you own ads on TV. This can be a dangerous activity for your business. It isn't that TV is more difficult than print or radio, the problem is the cost of a mistake. One mistake, your message in the wrong place or wrong target market can be very expensive.

Some final thoughts on TV

The most economical form of TV advertising is "spot" advertising. Local spots in your area are available on the Super Bowl. Not at hundreds of thousands of dollars for each minute but at local pricing based on viewership. The Super Bowl will be higher in price than normal local ads, but it may still be a bargain for you.

Keep in contact with your local sales rep for upcoming special programming that might attract your target market. Local sports is a great way to get some exposure for your business. Don't wait until your local team is ready for the Championship game to buy your spots. Make a deal at the beginning of the season that if the team reaches the finals and TV coverage is planned that you will commit to a certain number of spots. That way you'll be locked in and others will be locked out.

Run ads several times over a period of weeks instead of months.

Try and run commercials in the middle of the show rather than at the end of one show and the beginning of another.

If you are going to run several spots in the same evening or during the same show, have two or three variations of the same commercial ready so the audience won't get bored seeing the same message over and over.

 If you can afford TV in your market and you can make good spots, then use it. Nothing is more powerful for reaching large numbers of customers and building name recognition.

Yellow Pages

The most used way to find a service or business on a local level in the United States is by far the Yellow Pages. "Let your fingers do the walking", says it all. If you think you don't use the Yellow Pages that much, put it in the basement for a month and see how many times you reach for it. If you are in a service business: carpet cleaning, plumbing, carpentry or a contractor or electrician you'll get a lot of calls from the Yellow Pages.

For some unknown reason, the term Yellow Pages was never copyrighted by anyone, so you see it used by all sorts of local telephone directories. Here are the strengths and weaknesses of the Yellow Pages:

Strengths of the Yellow Pages:

Buyers: By the time a person gets to the Yellow Pages, they are already sold, they are looking for the place to buy.

Credibility: Most fly-by-night companies don't go to the time and expense of a Yellow Pages ad. If a company has a Yellow Pages ad, there is a perception, that company is probably honest and capable.

Classifications: If your business wears many hats, you can advertise under several headings. For example, a company that sells copy machines may also sell fax machines and would want to be under both listings and increase your customer base.

Free copy: Every person and business in your selling area that has a phone gets a free copy of your ad. Yellow Pages are used by 89.9% of all adults. It gives you total market coverage.

24 hours a day: It's ready to go and if you're a 24 hour business, customers are ready to buy.

Cost: The cost per thousand is relatively low compared to other media. (Remember to track cost per customer in your ad).

Extends the reach of other media: "See our ad in the Yellow Pages under widgets."

Yellow Pages Weaknesses:

Naked to the world: I turn to your Yellow Pages ad and there you are — with ALL your competitors. There is a chance I might call a company with a bigger ad, or one that says they provide the specific service I need.

Long lead time: You need to have your ad ready almost six months before the new phone book comes out.

No Updates: Change of address, phone, new services, discontinued services? Sorry, no updates until the new phone book comes out.

No Coupons: I was working with a video company in San Diego at the beginning of the video store boom in the early 1980's. We made the major mistake of putting a two-for-one movie rental coupon, with no expiration date, in our Yellow Pages ad good at any of the 15 stores we had at that time. This was during the early days when the average rental price was $5.00 per night.

People got coupons out of phone booths, offices, no phone book in the city was safe. For almost 18 month we gave away thousands of dollars in free movie rentals. It was a very painful lesson. Before you start to feel too sorry for us, we did go on to build 42 stores in San Diego and eventually sold the chain to Blockbuster Video for $12.5 million.

The final word on the Yellow Pages:

I think the consensus here is clear. If you can afford to be in the Yellow Pages, do it. When I first opened my marketing business in 1985, the profit from my first call paid for my Yellow Pages ad for the year. However, I placed a larger ad in a regional Yellow Pages and never received a single call from that ad. I'm not saying don't advertise in regional books, but you may want to ask similar businesses how their ads are doing. When in doubt, do what I did...Test an ad and find out. If it works next time buy a larger ad. Two good Yellow Pages resources to help you design and buy ads that work are: "Advertising In The Yellow Pages" by W.F. Wagner, and "Getting The Most From Your Yellow Pages Advertising" by Barry Maher.

Internet

The Internet itself is an entire book. Maybe my next book will be on this, it is a fascinating media. Here are just a few of the predictions of where it's going.

According to Dataquest (GartnerGroup Corporate Headquarters, 56 Top Gallant Road, Stamford, Connecticut 06904 USA +1-203-316-1111, a research firm), Internet connections increased 71% worldwide in 1997. The Internet population is expected to grow from 22 million in 1995 to 117 million by the year 2000. The World Wide Web (a segment of the net) will grow from 14.3 million in 1995 to 110 million by 2000.

Forrester Research predicts that by the year 2000 Internet-related services will generate $45.8 billion in revenue and an additional $46.2 billion in assets will be managed through the Internet.

Consumer Attitudes and Behaviors about the Net

Seventy-six percent of the U.S. public identify on-line services as "the wave of the future." (Project WOW!, 1995)

Twenty million of your friends and neighbors consider the Internet "indispensable." (Harper's Index, 1997)

Twenty-one percent of American households have access to the Internet (Internet World Magazine, February 1998)

How people learn about websites

Friends and other webpages (links): 96%

Magazines: 64%

Newsgroups: (People with similar interests that post information about their industries) :56%

Other sources: 36%
(Georgia Institute of Technology, 1995)

Fifty-one percent of U.S. adults think the Internet, e-mail and on-line "chatting" make people more social, while 41% say it makes them anti-social. (Luntz Research for Merrill Lynch, 1997)

Ninety-five percent of America On-Line users have purchased something from an on-line service. (Direct Marketing Association, 1997)

Percentage of consumers who own the equipment to get on line: 66%; spend at least 3 hours per week or more using on-line services: 35%; spend 3 hours or more per week using the Internet: 28%. (Metromail Corp, 1997)

How People View Internet Users

Trying to get ahead: 91%
Successful: 90%
Family-oriented: 78%

Similar to me: 76%
Nerds: 52%
Boring People: 35%
Couch Potatoes: 33% (Project WOW! Survey)

According to Commerce Net/Nielson, what business people are using the net for:

Gathering information: 77%
Collaborating with others: 54%
Vendor support and communication: 50%
Researching competitors: 46%
Communicating internally: 44%
Customer service and support: 38%
Publishing information: 33%
Purchasing products or services: 23%
Selling products or services: 13%

Profile of the average Internet User

(Source: Doublebase Mediamark Research Inc. 1997)

Males: 41.7% - Females: 58.3%
18-24 years old: 17.1%
25-34 years old: 28.0%
35-54 years old: 47.5%
55-64 years old: 5.6%
65+ years old: 1.8%

Professionals: 22.7%
Executives: 20.5%

Clerical/Sales: 27.3
Precision/Repair: 4.9%
Other: 11.2%

Homeowners: 69.9%

Post Graduate: 16.3%
College Degree: 47.7%
Attended College: 37.4%
Graduated High School: 12.4%
Did Not Graduate High School: 2.5%

Household income of $75,000: 40.2%
Household income of $60,000: 57.4%
Household income of $50,000: 67.9%
Household income of $40,000: 79.3%
Household income of $30,000: 87.9%

If you did your target marketing section correctly, you should be able to match up or not match up your target market with the average Internet user I've just profiled. I think it's interesting that the people with the household income that could most afford to use the Internet is the lowest group, (by percentage) in the profile.

Should you be on the net?

So, are you on the net yet? Do the prices of creating a web site scare you? If you aren't totally committed to this new medium yet here's some discussion to get you up to speed.

Do you sell to the world or do you do business locally? Local business can benefit greatly from a web presence if there are enough computers in your area. The cost can be prohibitive in some small towns.

If there is enough computer use in your area, you can put your brochure, catalog, price lists, maps and anything else you can think of on your page. Realtors, Travel Agents, Crafts, love web pages. Look at http://www.santalady.com for a global example and http://www.billiondeal.com for a local example.

Can you create your own web site? I created my entire site in Adobe PageMill 2.0. (160 page user guide and very easy to use) and software cost about $65.00. I created one simple page and took it to my Internet service provider (ISP) to make sure it would work before I did the whole site in this program.

The cost of the site at $60.00 per hour had I used a web page design service would have been approximately $6,500.00 to $10,000.00! A pretty good savings. Can't afford the software? Free web pages are available at: http://www.geocities.com and http://

www.cybertown.com. Finding ways of getting your message out while saving money is what we do here.

Am I a computer wiz? No, I'm a marketing wiz. The difference is, I sat down and forced myself to learn how to do a website.

Do you have the time to maintain the site and keep it up to date? Nothing will turn people off more than a site that never changes. Why keep coming back if there is no new information? If you're going to have a site you must make it interactive with your potential customers.

Here are a few strengths and weaknesses of the Internet:

Strengths of the Internet

Look, I'm BIG: You can look as big as Microsoft, Coke or anybody else out there. No one can tell by looking at a web page how big the company is.

Cost: (You'll find this in the negatives too) If you can create and maintain your own website (I did mine, so how hard can it be?) the cost is less than any other media. It is literally pennies for the vast numbers of potential customers you'll reach. No other media can reach the entire world 24 hours a day, 365 days a year with your message.

Size of your message: My website located at http://smalltownmarketing.com has 40 pages at present. By this time next year it will have well over a hundred. I recently read about a game magazine site that has over 600 pages. Some sites have over 5,000 individual pages. Try keeping those all linked together.

. If you have a catalog of products, where else can you have a full color catalog of your entire line available anywhere in the world? What is the cost of printing 1,000 full color catalogs? How about updating that catalog?

You can put your brochure on line. Moving images to demonstrate your product; sound, music,...if you can imagine it, it can be done on the net.

Compliments other advertising: Put your web address on every piece of literature you have. Business cards, stationary, brochures and every ad you run in any media. Does your local Chamber of Commerce have a website? See about a listing or banner. Use all your resources to direct people to your web site. Use your web site to call them to action and order your products.

Business Help: If you don't have a web site, or have no desire to have one, I would still encourage you to get Internet access at home or work. The amount of FREE helpful business information is overwhelming. The Small Business Administration has business plans and marketing information. Individual industries have web sites to help you with almost any question.

Weaknesses of the Net

Size: The very thing that makes the Internet so attractive to business is also one of it's biggest weaknesses. Twenty thousand sites per year join the Internet family. It is so big it's easy to be lost in a sea of information.

Cost: If you aren't able to create and maintain your own site the costs involved can be high. Website design can range anywhere from $30.00 per hour to several hundred dollars per hour. The Internet provider (think of it as the switchboard at the phone company) will charge a monthly fee for hosting your site. Usually this cost is based on the size (amount of computer memory required) of the site. The more space it requires the higher the cost.

ISP (Internet Service Providers): It never ceases to amaze me how people look at the cost of a service. I was talking to a businessman who was bragging about how little he was paying for his site.

ISP's are businesses just like any other, they need to show a profit to survive. The expense of an ISP is very, very HIGH. Will your low cost ISP be able to stay in business cutting their prices? Will they be able to maintain the equipment? The answer is usually NO. If they goes under then what?

If you can't get your site out of their system you may have to pay to create it all over again. In addition to that if you change providers, you can't use the same address. You'll need to put a "We've moved" page up to direct people to your new home.

Make sure you look at more than price when selecting an ISP. They must have the best available equipment, be up all the time, and operate flawlessly.

According to Boardwatch Magazine, there were 1,447 Internet Service Providers in February of 1996: in August 1997, there were 4,133. Be very careful in selecting an ISP. Price is the *very last* consideration I would have. Ask to speak with some customers who are doing well with the service. Talk to them and see if they are satisfied with the customer support.

Register a domain name

A domain name is a name you own and only you can use. For example, www.nbc.com is exclusive to the National Broadcasting Company. It will help your advertising greatly if you have either a distinctive or descriptive name. Something easy to remember. The address to register a domain name is: http://rs.internic.net/help/domain/new-domain-reg.html

My site name is www.smalltownmarketing.com. (if you just type smalltownmarketing.com, I'll come up). It's easy to remember and it describes what you'll find at the site. If I didn't have my own registered name my address would be: www.avicom.net/smalltownmarketing/index.html. How easy is *that* to remember? Leave out or mis-type any part and you wouldn't find me. This is a major problem with free page sites. The address must be in front of the customer. They couldn't possibly remember it.

Hits / Visitors: This is more a misunderstanding than a weakness. We read from time to time of a web site getting 1,000 hits a day or 10,000 hits a day or a 100,000.

What is a hit? Most people think it's a person who came to your site. No it isn't. A hit is an exposure to an element on one page of your site.

When a person visits your site and goes to a specific page on that site that is 1 hit. If the page has 3 graphic elements on it, each graphic on the page counts as a hit. So now our visitor has seen one page and we have 4 hits (one for the page and one for each of the elements). They move to the next page and bingo, 4 more hits and so on. If we have enough pages, and they stay long enough, they may do 1,000 hits by themselves.

There is nothing deceitful about telling folks your page is getting a lot of hits. Just make sure you aren't inferring that hits are individual visitors. New websites talk about hits and established sites with lots of traffic talk about unique visitors.

Search Engines: The most popular way for someone to find something on the Internet is to go to a "Search Engine." Type in a word, (such as "spider") and the search engine will find all the sites that deal with spider for you. Then you can scroll through the pages and pick a site by clicking on it. A point to remember when searching; If you enter the word "Coffee" with a capital "C", the search engine will only return pages that have Coffee with a capital C. If you enter the word "coffee", the search engine will return all instances of both "coffee" and "Coffee."

Websites are usually submitted to search engines by your ISP (Internet Service Provider). They have the knowledge and are familiar with the procedures. You can submit your site to some search engines yourself. One popular site is http://www.submit-it.com/. They will submit your site to a certain number of search engines free or more for a fee.

There are six major search engines. They are: Excite, Infoseek, WebCrawler, Lycos, AltaVista and HotBot. There is also one other, the most popular, called YaHoo! YaHoo is a special case because it's not a search engine at all. It's an index of sights in categories that is written and updated daily by editors.

So what's the weakness here? Try and picture yourself wanting some information and you went to a warehouse with one giant yellow page book with all the businesses in the world. How would you find what you're looking for? Find a heading and look at businesses alphabetically? How fair is that to people in the "Z's" Sorry, the net doesn't work that way.

A search engine looks at a combination of 5 things: There are other variables, but none as crucial as these five.

1. The title tag of the site. When my site comes up the title is "Small Town Marketing."

2. The first paragraph of the site's HTML (hyper text language) text.

3. The rest of the text on the pages.

4. The number and occurrence of certain words (marketing, for example). This entire book is on my site. If they are looking for marketing, I'm there! (Did I mention this is a marketing book about marketing.)

5. And for some, but not all, "meta" keywords and "meta" description tags. These are written in a specific way (by software or ISP programmers) so search engines can find them.

The weakness is that the importance of these five elements varies from one search engine to another. And they can vary from month to month.

Also notice, there is nothing about graphics in the five steps above. A site loaded with graphics is nearly invisible to a search engine. If you check out my site, you'll see graphics are at the bare minimum. Large graphics take time to load (come up on the screen). If your page loads too slowly, your customers will leave.

Last but not least, it can take anywhere from a few days to several months before your listing begins to appear on the search engines. YaHoo! receives over 8,000 submissions every day. If you have a site up and nothing is happening, maybe this is part of the problem. Be patient, they will start to show up and your traffic will increase.

Credit Cards: Are they safe on the net?: I go into a restaurant, enjoy a nice meal and give the waitress my credit card. She takes the card, processes it; at closing it goes to whoever makes the bank deposit, then to the bank to a teller, then to someone at the credit card clearing house, then to another teller at the issuing bank; to a dumpster in downtown Philadelphia and finally to a landfill. How safe is that?

This is so ridiculous I am reluctant to waste the paper to discuss it. The restaurant argument above is the very same one that went around when the first credit card was introduced in the mid 1960's. People were sure clerks in stores would steal the numbers and they would be liable for the purchases. People would never even consider giving a credit card number over the phone.

Do you really believe there is someone out there with the equipment needed and the expertise waiting to get your card number? To do what? Buy a Rolls-Royce? Most of us don't have a credit balance large enough to buy a tank of gas. If you want to tell me a hacker wants to break into CitiCorp and steal 10 million credit card numbers, that I'll believe before I'll believe they're laying in wait for me to make a transaction. If you are really concerned, get a credit card with a small limit and only use it on the net. Under current law you're only libel for $50.00 on a stolen credit card.

"Sorry, the system is down": Does your provider have multiple connections? For example, if they are exclusive with MCI and MCI goes down - guess what - *you're down too!!* With multiple connections you are protected from the failure of a single carrier. Ask.

The last word on the Internet

Internet commerce is on the move and you may want to consider being a part of it. Does promotion of your web site pay off? Consider this:

In 1994, for every dollar direct marketers spent on Internet advertising, $4 in sales were generated. By 1997, ad-to-sales ratios have almost doubled—for every dollar direct marketers spend in advertising on-line. On average, $7 in sales are generated, according to a report entitled "Economic Impact: U.S. Direct Marketing Today—A Landmark Comprehensive Study, 1997." I don't know about you but I could live with those numbers.

If you're interested, the study was commissioned by The Direct Marketing Association conducted by The WEFA Group. The complete study may be purchased by contacting the DMA's Book Distribution Center at 301-604-0187.

What can I say. The net is good, it's bad, and everything in between. I guess the question to ask, should you be on it? Here are some questions to ask yourself:

1.) Do you print and distribute large amounts of materials to customers?

2.) Do you provide documentation or specifications to customers?

3.) Would customer service and support costs be reduced if information was available on demand?

4.) Do you sell by direct mail or mail order?

5.) Can your business be easily described by a keyword?

6.) Do you ship products to customers?

7.) Do you sell directly to the customer?

8.) Is there something that makes your product unique?

9.) Can your product be easily shipped to a customer?

10.) Do you produce catalogs of merchandise?

If you answered yes to 8 or more, you should consider a net presence.

Summary of advertising in general

If there is one mistake small town businesses make more often than any other it's "What ever is left over, we'll use for advertising."
Marketing and advertising is an investment, not an expense. I know it sure seems like an

expense to me when I'm writing the check, but trust me it's not. Without enough money put aside for advertising your sales can go down and you suddenly have less and less to promote your business.

When do you advertise the most? For most businesses it's the first day of business. Don't you have a Grand Opening, balloons, flyers, ads, on-site radio remotes, contests, and prizes? Did the income from sales pay for that? No, it didn't. You have no sales yet. You advertise most when you need business. You advertise even more when you don't.

An average cost of advertising is usually 1 to 5% of gross sales, which can vary according to location, local advertising rates, and your particular industry. Car dealers need more advertising than funeral homes.

Let's look at the four basic strategies of successful advertising:

1.) In order to be successful, your advertising must provide a consumer benefit or solve a problem.

2.) That benefit or solution must be wanted by the consumer.

3.) The product or service you are offering must be tied directly to that benefit or solution.

4.) The benefit or solution must be distinctly communicated through media advertising. In other words, be clear, forget the advertising glitz and make sure the message isn't lost in the ad.

A small-budget advertiser doesn't have the "deep pockets" to develop big advertising campaigns. Sometimes you need to break the rules to be noticed. Avis did it by admitting they were "Number 2" in the car rental business and that campaign took them from 6th place to second place. When they stopped that campaign they dropped back to 6th again.

Budget conscious advertisers must achieve top results for their advertising dollar. Expand your dollars by adopting some creative techniques.

Here are 25 tips I've used over the years to help small businesses get a jump on the competition. I hope these will help you:

1.) Radio, newspapers and magazine specialists will frequently give free help in developing an advertising strategy. Things like demographic information, and money-saving ways to produce your ads etc.

2.) Place your ads in off-hours or in unusual locations for less. Many times you can still reach your target market with these spots. Instead of a one-time big splash ad, be consistent with frequent small ads that work. We did this with the video store in San Diego. Several small ads in each section of the paper.

3.) Monthly magazines sometimes have unsold ad space at the end of the month they will sell at a discount.

4.) If you have an 800 number, put it in every ad for immediate response and feedback. Also website and email addresses.

5.) Test advertising consistently in the classifieds. These ads may draw more customers than more expensive display ads.

6.) Can you barter for the cost of ad production? Maybe the newspaper needs painting in exchange for an ad about your paint store.

7.) Piggyback advertising are the ads you receive with your MasterCard bill. Is there someone in your town that sends out a lot of bills? Can you put a small flyer in with their bills and split the postage? Or pay a small fee? Help them pay the postage.

8.) Split advertising costs with the people who sell to you. Vendors and manufactures are always looking for exposure. Let people know you carry their products and have the vendor pick up part of the ad cost.

9.) Are there up-front advertising discounts for cash?

10.) Consider advertising in regional issues of national magazines. The costs are lower and you can still reach your target market. TV Guide is a good choice. It stays around for at least a week. Time, Newsweek, and US News and World Report may stay in local doctors offices for years.

11.) Share ad costs with neighbor business. Video stores and Pizza parlors are natural partners. Have coupons to each others stores or share the cost of flyers.

12.) Try reducing the size of your ad (not in the Yellow Pages) or length of your radio spots. A 60 second spot is not twice as much as a 30 second spot but you won't get twice as many customers for a 60 over a 30. Going with small ads or shorter spots will allow you to do more ads which normally pulls more customers. It's better to be there every day with small ads than every month with one big one.

13.) Develop tight production controls to minimize the need to reject finished ads. The message is more important than the messenger. Don't try to produce ads that win awards, produce ads that sell.

14.) Who are your very best customers? Aim your ads to talk directly to people like them.

15.) What will suppliers give you in the way of point-of-purchase materials (Posters, stand ups, handouts, etc.) Some have excellent display racks you can use.

16.) Some national chains like Coke and Pepsi provide outdoor signs for businesses. There are also indoor lighted signs you write on with special markers to advertise your special offers.

17.) Can you sponsor a community event? A fun-run, golf tournament, or other event that will be well publicized in the community. Your name may not be prominently displayed but sometimes the positive exposure in the community will bring in new customers.

18.) Small businesses can seldom afford saturation advertising. You must be selective in the media that reaches your customers. Pin your ad reps down and make them show you exactly how their media reaches your target audience.

19.) Exploit the media you choose. If your message is verbal, you don't need TV. Use the strengths of radio, billboards and newspapers to the fullest.

20.) Consider direct mail. A letter and brochure before customer contact can increase business. An IBM study concluded that selling time can be reduced from 9.3 to 1.3 total hours with direct mail advertising. A Sales and Marketing Executives International Study showed salespeople went from eight orders per 100 cold calls to 38 orders per 100 when direct mail was used.

21.) Try an editorial style ad. These are ads that look like actual stories in the newspaper. They will have "advertisement" shown at the top of the article. Develop a good headline, and 50% more people will read the article than would read an ad of the same size. Most will miss the word advertisement at the top.

22.) You can't match larger competitors dollar-for-dollar but, you can use unusual approaches (like the Avis idea), but color, music, slogans, humor (but be careful), or media selection to win your market away from the big guys.

23.) Due to the high costs of conventional advertising on radio, TV and newspapers, many cost-conscious business have been forced to look for lower cost methods. Can you advertise on parking meters, taxi boards, balloons, blimps and grocery shopping carts? Or on community bulletin boards, movie ads and weekly newspaper shoppers?

24.) Key your ads. Put something in the ad that will let you know which media it came from. On coupons, put a code that will record the paper and date of the ad. In radio or TV, have them mention the ad to get the discount. Ask every customer how they found you.

25.) Plan for a rainy day. During the year put a small amount aside each month for emergencies. You never know when you'll need to react quickly to whatever the competition is doing. You must be able to capitalize on breaking national events or news regarding your industry. If negative things happen in your industry you may need to respond quickly to make sure the right message is presented.

26.) Always give the customer more than you promised and more than they expected. This is tip number 26 of the 25 you expected. Maybe this last one is the one you needed.

I hope these tips will help your business grow. Not all may be relevant to your particular situation. Hopefully, they will illustrate the importance to plan and control your advertising budget.

One more time before we leave, Advertising and Marketing are what? Very good. An Investment -invest wisely and reap the benefits.

Publicity:

The last topic of the media mix is *publicity*. How to get it and how to use it. Here are some things you need to do immediately if you haven't already:

1.) Most newspapers have an "assignment editor", who assigns the stories to the reporters. Write him/her a letter explaining your expertise in your industry and that if a story about your industry comes along, you would be happy to provide information to them. Enclose a rolodex card with your name and address, phone, etc. If you don't have a rolodex card you can buy blanks at most office supply stores. If you can't find one enclose a business card.

2.) Contact civic groups in your area. Many have weekly or monthly programs. Most won't let you do an infomercial for your company but they will allow you to talk about your industry. For example, I've spoken at many of the Kiwanis Clubs in the San Diego area. What was my topic? "How to Market Your Kiwanis Club", of course. Do you have a fear of Public Speaking? We all do. Take a Dale Carnegie Course, that was my answer. Your local Adult Education Office may offer public speaking courses also.

3.) Most newspapers and magazines have what is called a "masthead" near the front of the publication. This will list the publisher, editor, and specific editors of various sections of the publication. For each publication and radio/TV station in your advertising area, start a record of the following: Name and title of the contact person; publication or station name; if radio, type of format (rock, talk, country); address, phone and zip code; the areas of interest they are responsible for (city news/county news/features/sports); publication demographics as they pertain to your business; deadline dates, if any; any past articles that have to do with your industry or business in general; any past articles about your competitors; and a record of all letters and discussions with each media.

4.) Have some press photos done. Always use a professional photographer. Don't save money by doing it yourself. Take pictures of your staff and key employees, your business, products or service (in use if possible, action shots sell), and your building or storefront if you have one. For your portrait shots use a light background if possible, it will reproduce better in the newspaper. If news breaks and you need to "seize the moment", you need to be ready with the info the media needs or they will find it elsewhere.

Press releases: What are they and how to use them?

Press releases are announcements sent to newspapers, magazines, radio and TV stations containing newsworthy information about your company, service or industry. They are written in a very specific format which I will cover in a moment. First, let's deal with the steps of preparing the information for a press release.

1. It must be news: No media is going to run a free commercial for you. There is a thin line where news ends and a commercial begins. The paper or station wants to stay on the news side and you want to be on the commercial side. If you can't explain why it's news then it may not be and they won't print it.

2. Who gets the release: Remember the list I asked you to make earlier. That's the group who gets the final version.

3. No more than three pages max: An editor may receive several press releases in a day. If the article is too long, it probably won't even be read. Be brief and to the point. Mark Twain is quoted as having said, "I'd have written you a shorter letter but I didn't have the time." Take the time to be concise.

4. Who, What, When, Where, Why and How?: The news release should answer all of the above. Who did what? Who does it affect? How does it affect them? Why does it affect them and not someone else? When will it affect them? Where will it happen?

5. Quotes: Experts in your industry add weight and credibility to the story but don't over use.

6. Can you write?: Many small businesses will have to write their own releases. If you don't feel comfortable writing the release yourself look for a professional to help. If none are available look to the English department at the nearest college or university.

7. Prepare a media kit: If there are studies, illustrations, pictures that support your story include them. They may not be used but if the story is used they will strengthen your position. Have all the photos, brochures, company history, past news articles, awards and anything else you can think of that will enhance your image in the eyes of the press.

8. Prepare your staff: There is nothing worse than having a reporter show up on the day you are gone and get some off-the-wall quote from one of the staff. Make sure people at your business either make an appointment when you can meet with the reporter, or have a designated spokesperson to act in your behalf who is familiar with the press release and what you want to accomplish. Make sure all employees are familiar with the media kit.

9. There are no guarantees: If the paper decides to run a story on you, there are no guarantees that it will appear when you want and where you want. Your story may be buried back by the classifieds somewhere. Worse yet, they may have gotten "the other side of the story" from your competitor. They may gloss over your best stuff and just print some statistics and not even mention your name.

10. Follow-up: For a newspaper, follow-up in one or two days. Don't ask, "When are you going to print my story?" Instead ask if there are any questions you can answer. Is there any additional information you might be able to provide?

What should a press release look like?:

A press release has a very specific format. Since this is a download type book, and some people are going to have to download a text only version, I will have to verbally describe the press release.

The cover page is usually on company stationary. If you don't have any, typeset the company name, address, zip and phone in the upper left hand corner of an 8 1/2 x 11 page. Margins should not be less than 3/4 inches or more than 1 inch from all sides. In the upper right hand corner type the following:

NEWS RELEASE
Contact for Editorial Information:
Your Name, Your Title
Phone Numbers

The first line flush left, all capitals should be:

FOR RELEASE ON (Insert date) or
FOR IMMEDIATE RELEASE

Next, announce the news with a clear simple headline, in upper and lower case type, centered on the page, such as:

NEW BOOK DETAILS MARKETING PLAN
FOR BUSINESS OWNERS IN SMALL TOWNS

Start the news with the location and current date. And the first paragraph would look like this:

Bozeman, Mont. - July 6, 1999 - Small Town Marketing.Com announced today a new book entitled "How To Market, Advertise and Promote Your Business Or Service In A Small Town" by Tom Egelhoff. The book is aimed at small businesses in locales where marketing and advertising agencies are either unavailable or not affordable. The book provides a step-by-step marketing plan designed for the special challenges of marketing a business or service in a small town. Also included are chapters on small town business promotion, small town advertising, small town success principles and homebased business success principles. This book is available for immediate download at http://smalltownmarketing.com.

Tell the story in the first paragraph

When you write the first paragraph, keep in mind that it may be the only part the paper uses. The first paragraph should be able to stand alone without any of the rest of the release. Use additional paragraphs for additional points in order of importance and priority.

Each paragraph is flush left, no indents, put a double space between paragraphs. If the release is going to continue to the following page(s) place the word (More) in parenthesis centered at the bottom of the page.

At the end of the release, put three number symbols centered on the page.

###

The news release alone is enough to write an entire book on. Visit the public library and you'll find several books on the subject. Check with the local newspaper. Sometimes they will have prepared a news release outline that details the way they would like to receive a news release.

A few points to keep in mind. Can you tie your business image to any national event? World Series, Olympics, or the Super Bowl? What about something going on in your state? Do you have an unusual product or service? Do any of your employees have a personal story that relates to your business?

Damage Control

There comes a time in every business when something negative will happen. As I mentioned, my parents were in the florist business. I remember a time when our dog bit a customer. Fortunately for my parents, this was during a time in the country when people weren't looking for a reason to sue each other. We treated her on the spot and gave her some free merchandise and an apology and that was the end of it.

In today's society, we would be looking at a significant law suit, the certain death of the dog, and possibly the end of the business.

You are never going to know what will happen or when. We couldn't have foreseen that dog bite, but we could foresee something like using pesticides on the flowers injuring someone, a delivery person hitting a pedestrian. I don't want you to get paranoid that you must consider every possible accident that could possibly happen in the universe. But, look at your business. Are there specifics of your business that could be a potential for bad publicity?

Many companies create hypothetical situations and create the necessary media response even though they have no reason to believe it will really occur. It's the boy scout motto: "Be Prepared."

The last word on publicity:

The advantage of a small town is you won't have several thousand businesses trying to outdo each other in the quest for news space. You'll only have a few hundred.

Take a good look at your business and what's going on around you and make some news.

Chapter Nine:
Step 8: Design A Marketing Calendar

Set up your marketing and advertising calendar

Now that you have all your marketing steps completed, it's time to set your calendar for the first six months of the year. By the first six months, I mean start *now*, don't wait until next January to start this.

Use a piece of 8 1/2 x 14 legal size graph paper with boxes that cover the page. 14 inch side will be the top. This size works best and is easy to file and work with. Divide the paper in half horizontally. Create a graph that shows the 52 weeks of the year across the top. On the left side of the top half, list the sales, promotions, or events your business has planned for the next six months. On the left side of the bottom half, list the various media you intend to use over the next six months. Radio, TV, newspaper, magazines, flyers, billboard, etc.

Now you can start to set up your calendar. If you are a retail store, list things like; half-off sale, anniversary sale, or Mother's Day sale down the top part of the left side. Let's say you have the half-off sale scheduled for the first week in March. Place your finger on "Half-Off Sale" on the top left side and move to the right across the graph until you are under March, place an X in the box for the first week of March.

Next, go to the second half of the page to the media you have listed. Let's say you will do some newspaper ads to promote your half-off sale. Let's also say, since the half-off sale will be the first week of March we want to promote the sale in the last week in February.

So, go down the left side of the page to newspaper, move to the right until you are under the last week in February and place an X in the box. If you have a spread sheet program like Excell or Lotus 1-2-3 this is easy.

What you want to be able to do with this calendar is go to any week of the six month period, start at the top and go down and see what promotions are coming up and what media must be contacted and ads prepared. Then what merchandise to order, what signs to have made, and how much advertising to budget each month, all on one sheet of paper that can be posted in your office. It also keeps employees updated on what's coming up so they can start promoting events to your customers.

This is a very important part of your total marketing plan. It will keep you on track and act as a constant reminder of where your business is and where you want it to go.

Chapter Ten:
Step 9: Execute Your Plan
Or Plan Your Execution

This will be the shortest chapter in this book. The title says it all. You have finished your marketing plan, now it's time to put it to work. You have your objectives, your target market, the types of promotion you will use, and the media you will use. All that remains is to execute the plan as you have designed it.

One point that should be made as you execute your plan, some things may not go exactly on schedule or happen as you hoped they would. Radio spots will be skipped, ads will be run wrong, or on the wrong days. Things like this will happen and as the plan is being executed, you need to be ready to react if something goes wrong. Anytime you place responsibility in the hands of anyone who doesn't have a vested interest in your business, Murphy's Law (Anything that can go wrong, will go wrong.) may take over. The best advice I can give you is be ready for anything.

Chapter Eleven:
Step 10: Is Your Plan Working?

The final step is perhaps the hardest of all. An honest and objective evaluation of how the plan is or is not working. When you are close to your business, and these are your ideas, and they aren't working, even though every fiber of your being says they should be, it's tough on some people's egos to regroup and try another direction.

Keep in mind that no one knows how the public will react to anything. The Pet Rock pretty well proved that. They should come to our store but they aren't. Why not? What have we missed? Chances are you haven't missed anything. The chances are you haven't waited long enough.

Marketing takes time to be effective. It is trial and error and testing, testing, testing. Most good marketing promotions take anywhere from six to nine months before results are noticed. You are asking people to do something new. Consider your product or service instead of what they usually do. That process takes time.

Talk to anyone who has run one newspaper ad one time and then tells you newspapers don't work—nobody came in. It's like playing baseball for the first time. You take one swing, miss, and then decide you can't hit so why play.

The best way to evaluate the plan is to do it in pieces, not as a total entity. Look at the various objectives you have set. Sales objectives: How are your salespeople doing? Are sales edging upward? Staying the same?

What about your marketing objectives and strategies? Are they on track? Is your positioning strategy working? Any feedback on pricing, packaging, or your brand name? Are you getting any publicity from your news releases? Are the advertising media producing any traffic? As you can see there are many areas in a marketing plan that must be evaluated before the plan is scrapped is favor of something else. Your plan will be in a constant state of evolution as you evaluate and improve the various components. Don't panic if results aren't immediate. The sales of this book weren't immediate. The marketing plan has to grow. It starts as an infant and grows into a self-sustaining entity.

Section Two:
Small Town Success Principles

The very strength of a small town is the key to your success in it. What is the strength of a small town you ask? It's people. Small towns have people, large cities have numbers, constituents, inhabitants—they are the public. People in small towns not only know each other, they go out of their way to meet each other and introduce their friends to others. If you are a "people person" you will have a tough time failing in most small towns.

Small town people were "networking" with each other long before is became the buzzword of the 90's. Small town people are forced to know each other by county fairs and church socials, funerals, their kids, civic events and town meetings. They also understand that, in many cases, they are going to be together for a long time. Most of these folks would hate city life. Given a choice of living in New York for the same price as their small town, for most folks its a no-brainer. They might like to visit New York—But Live There? Not a chance.

If you are just moving to a small town here are some things to do to help your success:

1.) Start meeting people. The local churches are the best place to start. These folks will welcome you with open arms. If they don't, then it's not really a church, is it?

2.) You are in business, where do the business people meet? In the small town of Jerseyville, Illinois, where I grew up, a group of business people used to meet every morning at a big round table in the back of one of the local restaurants. In Bozeman, where I live now, the local Rotary Club, Lions Club and Kiwanis Club have a lot of the movers and shakers in town. The Chamber of Commerce has "Business After Hours" meetings once a month that are very popular with business people. Join these groups and meet people.

3.) If you have a problem meeting people, find the friendliest folks you can and build on them. Ask them to introduce you to some of their friends. And ask those friends and so on and so on.

4.) Many successful business people are happy to share their good fortune with the community by their involvement in the United Way or Scouting. These groups are usually supported by the better and more successful businesses in town. Join these groups and let them know, you also, are a person who wants to help your new community.

If you are long established in your community here are some things you can do to add to your success:

1.) Become the new welcome wagon for your town. By that I don't mean go around with gift baskets and welcome each new resident. When new businesses open or people are in your town "scouting" for a business location, meet as many as you can. They are your new customers.

2.) Support and encourage those around you. Whether you are the boss or the employee you'll go farther as either with this attitude.

3.) Be as optimistic as possible all the time. You'll find if you do this it's contagious. It's easy to sit around and gripe about everything in your life going wrong. Nobody wants to hear it. Be positive and customers and employees will see you as positive and they will follow you.

4.) Show courage in your business and your personal life. We don't name highways or build statues to cowards. Be a leader in your community.

5.) Don't be afraid to seek the advice of others (provided they are qualified to give that advice).

Don't ask some guy you just met in a bar to evaluate your business. Be selective in who you ask for help.

6.) Always act, think, and talk like a professional. You will never be one unless you can see yourself as one. When we look at someone, we can't see their pedigree. We don't know what we're getting until we see some positive sign that shows this person is OK. What do you call a person who got the lowest passing grade in medical school? You call him Doctor.

As you walk or drive around your small town tomorrow, take a really good look and appreciate what you have. Then set your sites on making it better. The rewards you receive will be 100 fold.

Section Three:
Small Town Advertising

I covered the basics of advertising extensively in the Media Mix Chapter of the marketing plan. What I want to do here is touch on a few points that are specific to small towns and some final points to keep in mind as you put the word out to the world.

1.) Big city messages don't often work in small towns, so be careful of using pre-made ads from large companies. An ad that shows a family on the front steps of a New York City brownstone may work great there, but no one in Judith Gap, Montana is going to relate to it. Use the idea of these ads and have them redone with a farm family on the back steps and you'll have a winner.

2.) Small towns are people. In your ads, speak directly to one of those people, not the whole town. Each person will feel you are speaking only to them.

3.) Small town people are often portrayed as backward hicks or uneducated. They aren't. They are you. And you must be truthful and absolutely believable in your ads if you want their business.

4.) Screaming and yelling may be effective in larger cities but seldom works in small towns.

5.) Talk is cheap. If your product is good you're going to have to prove it here.

6.) Many small towns have retired folks and senior citizens. Make sure your ads are readable to these people. Type should not be smaller than ten point (12 point or larger is preferable).

7.) Small towns are bombarded by telemarketers just like large cities. You may want to consider a coupon or a return card with your ad instead of an 800 number. Studies have shown many people feel they are going to get a "high pressure" sales pitch at the 800 number.

8.) Unlike a large city, small towns have more general demographics. A large city may have a large area of Eskimos you want to reach. You may want to create an ad just for them. In a small town your message must be more consistent in the different media you use or it can be lost in the clutter.

9.) Testimonials are very powerful in small towns. If you can get an influential local person to endorse your product or service, your competitor is out in the cold. He'll have to find another influential person to combat yours. In a small town that's not always easy to do. Line up several people, if you can, and shoot the commercials as fast as possible. They can be released slowly over a long period of time.

10.) Keep every promise you make. Keep them even if you didn't make them. I tell the story of the lady who returned the set of tires to Nordstrom's. Nordstrom's doesn't sell tires, they sell clothes. They took the lady's tires and cheerfully refunded her money. This kind of service separates them from their competitors.

Advertising in a small town is dealing with real, honest, sincere people. They haven't been corrupted by the cutthroat tactics often used in the big cities. They look for the best in people and expect the same in return. If you plan to do business in a small town give your customers the level of service you'd expect. You'll be glad you did.

Section Four:
Small Town Promotion

How to bring them in

When you think of a promotion, most people think they're going to get something free. That isn't always the case, but people view a promotion as something good.

Who does promotions? Car dealers are probably the world champs, followed closely by Circuit City® type stores, and finally furniture stores. Why promote? It gets people in your store in a buying frame of mind. So what makes small town promotion any different than anywhere else?

The main difference is population numbers versus the cost of the promotion. A large city promotion may draw thousands while a small town promotion may only draw a few hundred. What those few hundred actually purchase may not even cover the cost of the promotion, much less leave a profit. Any promotion is tricky but small town promotion is even more dangerous.

Why do a promotion? What is the objective that you want a promotion to accomplish? One reason might be to stimulate business during a slow time of the year. Perhaps a Christmas sale in June might draw some attention. If you are introducing a new product or service to the community. Show off the new facility after a move or remodel.

When considering a promotion, the first item of business is almost always cost. How much is it going to cost us to "buy" these customers? And, make no mistake about it, you are buying them. You are giving them either a value or the chance at a value (such as a raffle).

The least expensive promotion, in my opinion, is the cross-promotion. Get together with a non-competing business and share the cost of the promotion advertising. This way you bring customers into both locations at half the cost.

Depending on your products, a drawing is probably the next best. Perhaps the manufacturer of the grand prize would be willing to provide some co-op advertising help. Be careful here, you may not see the co-op money for some time.

The most important thing about any promotion is proper exposure of your business or service to the right customer. There is nothing worse than spending a bundle in advertising, then seeing your store so full of customers that no one can even move much less see anything.

You can't always control the amount of people you're going to draw, but be prepared to move them through your business in an orderly and efficient manner.

Also remember, it's OK to sell things during a promotion. Sometimes business owners get so caught up in the celebration of the moment they forget that it's a business, it's OK to make a little money. Give them the store tour another time. Put them in front of the merchandise and close the sale.

Holding a drawing is a great way to generate a mailing list. I know what you're thinking, "That's pretty underhanded, don't you think?"

Keep in mind that these people are at the promotion because they have an interest on what's going on there. They may not be buyers today but keeping them informed with mailings may turn them into buyers in the future. Everyone likes to save money. Many of them will appreciate knowing about upcoming sales and promotions in the future.

The main point of promotion I want to make clear is, make sure you know what your objective is. What do you want the promotion to accomplish? Set a measurable goal. Is it the number of customers you attract? The amount of sales? An increase in sales from current customers to create increased sales after the promotion? All of the above?

Set goals and measure what happens. If the promotion is successful, you may want to run it again later in the year. Promotions help maintain a customer interest in your business. Good luck with yours.

Section Five:
Homebased Marketing Success Principles

The scenery never changes

Homebased businesses are vastly different than storefront type businesses, in that, you are always at home. The scenery never changes. You get out of bed and walk a few steps and you're at work. There are good and bad points to this arrangement.

Discipline yourself at home

Self discipline is the heart of success in my opinion. If you can't make yourself do the work and ignore the little outside things that interfere with your goals, you will not be a success in any field. The key ingredient to that self discipline is your dream or goal.

Successful people are successful because they have a dream or goal and they will not be denied in their quest to make that goal or dream a reality. They work unbelievable hours, overcome hardships and set backs and persist, no matter what.

Every successful person from Bill Gates to Mother Theresa got to where they are because they had the vision to see the goal and work toward it one step at a time, one day at a time.

Three Steps to Success

In this section of the book I want to cover the areas you need to recognize and deal with to make your business a success. There are three initial areas. They are: 1. Forced Discipline, 2. Associations, 3. Vision of the Future. Lets take them one at a time:

1. Forced Discipline. To understand forced discipline we must first understand the major differences between fear and desire. Fear is an extremely powerful motivator and inhibitor. Fear will keep you from achieving your goals. Desire will propel you toward your goal.

Fear of failure.

In his book, "The Psychology of Winning", Dr. Dennis Waitley, Ph.D. uses the following example. Suppose I placed a board two feet wide and fifteen feet long on the floor. I put a $100.00 bill on one end and asked you to walk the length of the board and pick up the $100.00 bill, would you do it? Of course you would. There is nothing to fear. Odds of failure are almost nil.

Now suppose I put one end of the board on top of a twenty story building and the other end on an adjacent twenty story building. I'll put a rock on the $100.00 just to make sure it doesn't blow away. Now would you walk the board? What have we added here? There is a very high penalty for failure isn't there. Twenty stories straight down. The $100.00, is suddenly, not a sufficient reward for the task that is asked.

Studies show more people fear public speaking than fear death. We fear what our friends will think of us, so strongly, it affects our morals, standards and principles. The fear of business failure and our friends laughing at us if we fail, stops most people from even considering starting a business.

This isn't high school anymore folks. If these people aren't helping you put food on the table for your family and don't support and encourage you, they aren't your friends. It's that simple. Lose em! I guarantee if you're successful they'll be gone anyway. They aren't going to hang around with a successful person and have to explain why they aren't successful. It just isn't going to happen.

People who make $100,000 a year don't hang around with people making $18,000. So get on with the only life you'll ever have and start making something happen for you and your family.

Desire - Just do it

Desire on the other hand is just as powerful as fear, but in a different way. Desire fights fear. When I was about 6 years old, I was at a swimming pool with my parents. I was playing in the shallow end of the pool and I suddenly slipped on the bottom of the pool and went under. From that day on I had a terrible fear of water. I never went into the water for any reason. You can imagine growing up in a farm community where every one had a pond or some body of water nearby. It was years later when I was in high school when I finally learned to swim and my fear of water miraculously went away. I thought to myself how stupid I had been. And all the fun I had missed by not taking the steps to overcome my fear.

My desire to learn to swim and be with my friends (girls primarily) finally pushed me to the point I had to overcome the fear. Desire was the answer. Once my desire became more powerful than my fear, the fear disappeared and my goal was achieved. That is also how business success is achieved.

Let's get back to forced discipline and you'll see how this all comes together. Forced discipline is fear. Self discipline is desire. Here's how they work:

As a kid growing up we lived under the shadow of forced discipline. Our parents made all decisions for us, and if we didn't abide by those decisions, there were consequences. "Clean up your room or you can't go out and play." "Mow the yard or no car this weekend." "Be home by midnight or you're grounded." At school, "Do your homework or you won't pass". At work, "Be on time or you're fired." "Your evaluation was low, no raise for you till you get the scores back up." "I've got my eye on you." Most people will stay where they are, in a job they despise, than face the fear of finding something better or more rewarding that may not work out. Better to stay with a sure thing than have no job at all.

The government, "Pay your income, property, sales, estate, excise, federal, state, city, county, and gas taxes or it's jail for you."

Is it any wonder we let fear overpower us? It's a life long habit we've acquired. Fear is quite literally a way of life for most people. Go through your normal day tomorrow and see how often you must confront and overcome fear.

Forced discipline is easy. You have no choice in most cases. Fear is always an easy excuse. That's why the majority of the American workforce spends all its time making someone else's dream come true instead of their own.

Self discipline, on the other hand, works to overcome the lifetime habit (and fear) of forced discipline. It's the only way to overcome it.

If you want to own your own business, you must have self discipline. There is no other way. You must have a goal and work toward that goal every day. The goal or desire must be the total focus of your life in order for you to be successful. In some cases, this may take a toll on your family. The extra hours of starting and running a part time business is going to infringe on their time. Writing this book took time away from my family. I didn't wait until everyone in the house was asleep to begin writing. When I decided to write this book I sat down with my wife and outlined the sacrifices we would both have to make in order to make the book a reality. I had to set a writing schedule and with few exceptions I stuck to it. Here is a short example of how I used self discipline to write this book:

Self Discipline Plan

Goal One: What is the result I want? Sell 5,000 copies of this book. In order to even write the book you must have a goal of what's going to happen when it's done. I wrote down exactly what I wanted and expected from this book. I see, in my mind every day, 5,000 books sold.

Goal Two: What am I willing to give in return for the 5,000 books sold. I am willing and will spend at least 15-20 hours a week writing and researching for as long as it takes. In this case about three years

Goal Three: Establish an exact date for goal number one. In this case, New Years Day, 2000. By setting this date in my mind, my subconscious mind will work every day to make that date happen. I will be pushed to market, advertise and do whatever is necessary to have 5,000 books sold by New Years Day, 2000.

Goal Four: I created a definite plan of how I was going to sell those books. I wrote a complete marketing, promotion and advertising plan to make my dream happen.

Goal Five: I wrote out a clear concise statement of the first four goals in as much detail in possible.

Goal Six: I read the statement created in goal five every morning and every evening. As I read the goals, I saw in my mind that they had already happened.

This is how self discipline really works. Your subconscious mind can't tell the difference between what is real and what is vividly imagined.

Don't we create imaginary fears in our minds? If we do, then why can't the opposite be true? If we imagine positive successful things, our minds will go in that direction, and we will work toward fulfillment of those commands.

Desire for success is the only way to overcome fear of failure.

Associations

It was the best of times, it was the worst of times. Excuse me as I paraphrase Charles Dickens, "Tale of Two Cities". For purposes of this book, let's change the quote slightly to, "They were the best of people, they were the worst of people." In a small town or in the relatively small world of the home based business we know a lot of people. Strange as it may seem a lot more people know us.

There's good news and bad news. The good news is, the expertise of people who know your field or can help you, probably will. The bad news is, people with absolutely no expertise about your business who couldn't possibly help you, probably will.

Friends or Foes

Remember the old saying, "Birds of a feather, flock together." We tend to associate with people who think the same way we do. Smokers gravitate toward each other, bowlers, golfers, hunters, readers, bird watchers, gang members, all "flock" together. So, are friends bad? No, friends aren't bad, unless they try to give you information they are unqualified to give.

If you want to learn to play golf, do you join the local bowling league and start asking bowlers about golf? There may be some golfing bowlers but doesn't it make more sense to go to the golf course, ask to see the golf pro, and take some lessons? Does it matter that the golf pro may be a complete stranger to you? The golf pro has the needed knowledge to assist you in accomplishing your goal...how to play golf.

Would you ask a friend who has never played golf before in their life to teach you. Why not? They're your friend aren't they? They have your best interest at heart, don't they? They want to see you succeed, don't they? Do you see where we're going here? The road to the hot place is paved with good intentions.

When my father decided to start his floral business, he drove to the next town, met florists, made friends, and hung around as long as they would let him. He watched how they designed things, what they charged, who the suppliers were and how they ordered products. He learned from people doing what he wanted to do.

Some people he didn't ask: his father, his brother, his sister, his best friend. The reason he didn't ask any of them? ...they weren't qualified to advise him. They, as he, had no experience in the floral business. Asking them would be a waste of time.

But, I always ask my father...

I know, I know, you always get your dad's advice in every major decision. When I bought my first car I asked my dad for advice. He had bought a lot of cars. He had more experience than I did in that area. Same with our first house. But for legal advice, guess what, he recommended an attorney to me. He didn't try to give me legal advice. He knew he wasn't qualified to do that. Even your best friends will tell you, "Get a lawyer and sue the SOB." They don't say, "Let's go to court, I'll represent you."

Doesn't it seem strange that with something as serious as your business, the way you provide for your family, that your friends are more than willing to explain to you why your business ideas won't work. Worst of all, they do it under the guise of saving you from yourself. "We don't want to see you go down in flames." Of course, they don't know anything about your business, how it works, or your vision for it. They can't see it so it can't possibly work.

Look at any great leader of business or industry and I'll guarantee you somewhere in this person's life they were ridiculed and laughed at by people who didn't understand their vision.

Whether you love him or hate him, Bill Gates is a perfect example of a man with vision who rejected family advice, endured all the computer nerd jokes, to rise to the pinnacle of his industry. I can imagine the IBM boardroom after signing the licensing contract with Gates for the DOS operating system. "Well I hated to take advantage of that young man", they probably said. In fact when Gates arrived for his first interview with IBM, he was so young looking, he was mistaken for a mail boy and sent to the mail room in the lower areas of the building.

If you feel you must ask your friends for their advice or opinions then do so. However, make sure you also get some advice and opinions from people who have done what you want to do. Ask someone who's been there. They will give you the good and the bad. Then you can make a qualified decision and move your business forward.

Vision of the Future

The third area of homebased business success principles is being able to see into the future. None of us truly knows what's around the next corner. Otherwise why would the Psychic Friends Network have to ask for your credit card number? Shouldn't they know that already?

If you are a parent, think back to when your children were about 6 months old. You're watching them crawl around on the living room floor. Do you picture them at 30 still crawling around in diapers? Probably not. You picture them educated, with promising careers, happily married with the world at their feet. Every decision you make, as they grow, is based on where you want them to be as an adult. Start picturing your business as your child. What do you see as its' future?

The Future Is NOW

I know it's hard when you look over in the corner of the room and there's a card table and a telephone and that's your business. Pretty hard to picture a threat to IBM isn't it? You need to get over that kind of thinking and do it now— The future is *today*. Your child didn't become an adult in a day and the same will be true with your business.

The second area of concentration is to reprogram your mind to see the business as you want it to be every time you make a decision regarding your business. "How will this decision affect my business 5 years, 10 years, 20 years from now?"

What is the destination?

An airline pilot flying from New York to London can't see his destination for almost 99% of his flight. The secret is knowing what you want the business to be, a plan to make it happen, knowing where the destination is...and moving toward it. Success has been defined as:

The progressive, day by day, realization of a worthwhile goal or dream.

Move day by day toward the dream or goal of your business, seeing your business as you want it to be and act like it's already there. Let me repeat that. *Act like it's already there.* Every decision, every sale, every contact says to clients and customers, this is a business on the grow. See your business, see the future.

Around the house...

If you've never had a homebased business before, here are a few points to keep in mind.

1. If customers come to your home for your service make sure it's the kind of place they want to come back to. For example, if you smoke, stop, or start smoking outside. Nothing will turn some customers off faster than stale smoke smell. The front yard. Keep it mowed, trimmed and as well manicured as possible. You should have the best looking yard on the block. Your front door. Get a nice looking front door, a small expense. If you can't paint the whole house, paint the front and tell customers you are in the process of painting the rest. No weird colors. Make sure the room customers enter from the outside is neat and clean. If they have to walk through the house make sure they are walking through clean rooms.

2. Dress. "Hey! One of the reasons I wanted to work at home is so I wouldn't have to dress up anymore!" Dress says who you are and what you think about your business and yourself. Dress says I'm a success, even if I work at home I'm still a professional. Dress doesn't necessarily mean a coat and tie or a dress and heels. It means neat, clean and professional. Put yourself in the customers shoes. Is the business in this house a business I want to deal with? Do I want to give this person my money? Am I confident that this business can do the job?

Remember, working out of your house has the stigma of not being as good as a storefront business. Although this attitude is becoming less and less prevalent as more and more people work at home.

3. Kids. There is only one answer for kids. Shoot em. OK, OK, don't shoot em. Remember the old saying, Children should be seen and not heard. This is a business statement etched in stone. Children should not come in contact with your customers...period. Children do not go to work with their parents in conventional storefronts and the same should apply at home.

If you need to meet with clients for extensive periods, arrange for someone to come in to handle the children or arrange for their care somewhere outside the home. Don't assume that your customers probably have kids and they'll understand.

Look At Me

I'll never forget going to a house in a nearby town to look at some crafts a woman was selling. It was beautiful work but as soon as we walked in the door, her three children began yelling, running, asking us who we were and what were we going to buy. "Look at me." one said as he tried to climb up the wall. It was a nightmare. We did place an order and I dreaded having to come back to pick it up. I wanted to have the check already written and to leave as quickly as possible. Don't get me wrong, kids are great. They're God's greatest gift. You're used to them and how they act. Yelling and running is the normal things your kids do. To other people these activities are like fingernails on a blackboard. Unless it's absolutely impossible, keep kids out of business situations.

4. Phone. While we're on the subject of kids. If they answer the phone, teach them to do it in a professional manner. "Who is this?" "My name is so-and-so and I'm three." is not very professional. If you have one line into the house, make sure everyone who answers the phone knows a potential customer may be on the other end at any time. If you have two lines, make sure only you or designated persons answer your business line.

5. Fax Think you don't need a fax machine? Consider the following. Contact customers and ask if they would like to be notified of certain changes in the company. Faxes are a very inexpensive way to contact current customers about prices changes, new products and other information. One call can reach several customers using broadcast fax technology.

Use the fax as a substitute for the phone. Long distance and fax rates are lower after 5 p.m. and before 8 a.m.. Send faxes during these hours and save money. If you live on the East Coast you can reply to a client or customer on the West Coast, who simply needs a yes or no answer, after 5 p.m. (at lower rates) and its still mid-afternoon out West. You can place orders to suppliers this way too.

6. Image. In the past 10 years a new industry has emerged...the image makers. These are people who are paid to make sure people and companies put their best foot forward in the business community. You probably don't need one of these folks yet, but you do need an image.

Image is easy on the Internet. Some kid in his bedroom can look and sound as big and good as IBM or any other big company. With $65.00 worth of software and a few key strokes anybody can be a force on the net.

If you aren't on the net, that's OK. Look into the best stationary and business cards you can afford. If that's black ink on white paper, do it. You don't need fancy logos or unusual typestyles. Keep it simple. Make sure that if you need to send a letter to a supplier for credit or a customer regarding payment that you look professional.

Brochures

If you have brochures make sure they tell your story briefly but with enough detail to make the customer hungry for more information. If price is a consideration, qualify people asking for information. Contact them by phone and make sure they are legitimate customers and not just someone collecting information who may never buy anything.

Send postcards to potential customers with "Address Correction Requested" under your return address. Postcards cost one cent less than bulk mail. There is no minimum that can be mailed. They are delivered First Class instead of three to four weeks with bulk mail. You will receive corrections to your mailing list free of charge. Bulk mail will cost .32 cents for every card returned with a corrected address. Once your mailing list is clean. Send brochures with the confidence that they will reach the person they are supposed to.

Making a homebased business a success is one of the hardest jobs anyone can undertake. Many people will dismiss your job as a "hobby" and not really legitimate. Others will make fun of you and make it a point to ask, in front of others, if you've made your first million yet.

You have made the first steps in starting something they can only dream about. That dream will never come true for them because they fear the one thing that will bring them success.: taking the first step, and then the second, and the third.

You are taking those steps now. Don't look back, they will all be out of sight soon

Some Final Thoughts

Well, congratulations, you've persevered to the very end. It's that kind of resolve that makes successful people who they are. If I have any last words of encouragement, they might be a quote from one of my favorite books, "Think and Grow Rich" by Napoleon Hill (Ballantine Books ISBN #0-449-21492-3) He claims, "Every adversity, every failure, and every heartache carries with it the SEED of an equivalent or GREATER BENEFIT.". In other words, build on your mistakes. Measure and improve with growth and you are unstoppable.

Thanks for taking the time to read this book. I sincerely hope the tips and ideas I've presented will help you build a successful and profitable business.

I'd really like to hear about your business successes and challenges.
e-mail me at tommail@smalltownmarketing.com

Visit the Small Town Marketing Website at:
http://www.smalltownmarketing.com

Or write to:
Tom Egelhoff
Small Town Marketing
P.O. Box 271
Bozeman, MT 59771-0271

Worksheet For
Chapter Two: Business Resume

1. How Long In Business? _____

2. Business Experience (pg 22) _____

_____

_____

_____

3. The business principals are: (pg 22) __

_____

_____

_____

4. Special Skills: (pg 22) _____

_____

_____

5. Purchase Rates/Buying Habits: (pg 23)

_____

_____

6. Awareness/Product Attitude: (pg 23) _

_____

_____

_____

Worksheet For
Chapter Two: Business Resume
(Continued)

7. Competition: (pg 23) _____

_____

_____

_____

8. Pricing: (pg 24) _____

_____

_____

9. Target Market: (pg 24-27)

Age: _____

Sex: _____

Marital Status: _____

Own Home: _____

Children: _____

Income: _____

Education: _____

Newspapers/Radio etc: _____

_____

Worksheet For
Chapter Two: Business Resume
(Continued)

10. Demographics: (From Chamber of Commerce/Census:: _____

_____

_____

_____

_____

11. The end users of my products are: _

_____

_____

12. I will use these methods to distribute my products or services: (pg 27) _____

_____

_____

13. I will use these methods to sell my product: (pgs 31-52) _____

_____

_____

_____

Worksheet For
Chapter Two: Business Resume
(Continued)

14. Who can I contact who is successfully doing what I want to do?:

_____

_____

_____

_____

15. Where is my competition advertising?

_____

_____

_____

_____

16. I will complete this business resume on or before:

Date: _____

Signed: X _____

Witnesses: _____

_____

Worksheet For
Chapter Three: S.W.O.T. (pg 29-30)

1. . The strengths of my business are: __

_____

_____

_____

2. The weaknesses of my business are: _

_____

_____

_____

3. These are my opportunities for success:

_____

_____

_____

4. These are the threats to my business
success:_____

_____

_____

_____

Worksheet For
Chapter Four: Sales Forecasting

1. My sales objectives are: (pg 53) _____

_____

_____

_____

_____

2. My short term (1-year) goal is: (pg 53)

_____

_____

_____

3. My long term goal (3-5 years) is: (pg 53) _____

_____

_____

_____

4. My sales projections are: (pg 54-59) _

_____

_____

_____

Worksheet For
Chapter Six:
How To Create A Plan And Work It

1. These are my marketing objectives:

_____

_____

_____

_____

_____

2. These are my marketing strategies:

_____

_____

_____

_____

3. My competitive strategies are: _____

_____

_____

4. My pricing strategies are: _____

_____

Worksheet For
Chapter Eight: What do we say, how do we say it and where do we say it?

1.. Direct mail: (pg 95) _____

_____

_____

2. Co-op advertising: (pg 111) _____

_____

_____

3. Newspapers: (pg 112) _____

_____

_____

4. Magazines: (pg 119) _____

_____

_____

5. Radio: (pg 122) _____

_____

_____

6. TV: (pg 128) _____

_____

If you enjoyed this book, get
Tom's Second Book

"The Small Town Advertising Handbook: How to say more and spend less!"

Order Yours Today!!
Toll Free 1-888-550-6100 or

Please mail (   ) autographed copy(s) to:

Name:_____

Address:_____

City:_____ St:____ Zip_____

Credit Card Orders Must Include The Following:

Full Name: _____
(as it appears on card, or if different than above)

Address: _____City_____ St._____ Zip_____

Card Type: *(Visa, MasterCard, American Express, Discover)*:_____

Card Number:_____Exp Date:_____

Phone:_____

Or, mail check, money order, for $19.95
plus $4.00 shipping and handling for each copy to:

Smalltownmarketing.Com
P.O. Box 271 • Bozeman, MT 59771-0271